Mexican Cooking
made easy
including Latin American & Caribbean recipes

80-- 133843

Galahad Books • New York City

Mexican Cooking made easy published by Galahad Books,
New York City

This edition published by arrangement with 'Round the World
Books Inc., New York, New York

Series designed by Margaret Verner

Pictures on pages 12, 14 and 20 courtesy of the Mexican National
Tourist Council, Toronto, Canada.

Library of Congress Catalog Card Number: 79-87994

ISBN: 0-88365-418-0

Printed in the United States of America

Contents

The food of Mexico, Latin America & the Caribbean

INTRODUCTION

Who can think of the southern hemisphere and not immediately envision bright flowers and flags; hear soft-strummed guitars and deep, musical voices; see dark-eyed señoritas in bright swirling skirts dancing in the plaza or walking sedately through a paseo? Yet color and romance are not the only qualities of life there. Look south of our borders and you will discover a whole world of cooking which, through the centuries, has developed the idea that even the simplest foods can be stimulating and satisfying as well as basically nutritious and economical.

Here, the Indians of the ancient Mayan and Aztec civilizations perfected a sophisticated cuisine thousands of years before the arrival of the first Europeans on their shores. The natural plenty of the lands was skillfully enhanced and cultivated to provide a rich, spicy, sound diet for the people who lived in the vast areas extending through Mexico and Central America many thousands of miles to the southernmost tip of the peninsula of South America. Corn, beans, tomatoes, potatoes, squash, peppers, chocolate, bananas and avocados, as well as exotic fish and fruits, were the basis of the great Indian cuisines, and their intensive cultivation helped develop new and better strains of all the native vegetables. In certain areas wild game was plentiful. And in the mountainous countries a process of freeze-drying was in use from the very origins of life on the continent.

When the first Spaniards arrived in Mexico, they were treated to the sight, and taste, of royal banquets literally "fit for the gods." They soon discovered that one of the great riches of the New World was its natural bounty.

There exist, today, descriptions of the feasts prepared for the Inca, the head of that great state on

6

Fish is dried in the sun and sold in the open market of Tempico

An infinite variety of ground chilies, dried beans and cornmeal form the foundation of many Latin American dishes.

the West Coast of South America, where as many as five hundred different dishes were prepared for his choice! This is even more incredible when one considers that there were almost no fresh meats as we know them, nor any fats or dairy products, since domesticated animals were such a rarity. Most of the food was boiled, steamed or roasted – frying was virtually unknown.

For great fiestas, the barbecue was developed. The clam-bake which we associate so much with New England is actually an adaptation of this most ancient Indian form of cooking. A large hole is dug in the ground and a fire built in it. When the fire has diminished to a huge bed of hot coals, the pit is lined with leaves, then food is set in it – a whole animal in its own hide is added. (Barbecue means, quite literally, from "beard to tail.")

Vegetables and pots of stews etc. are placed around, then all is covered with more leaves, more

mud and more fire and left to bake for the required time. The pit is broken open and the deliciously steamed food served to all. This method is still used today, not only for the New England clam bake, but the Hawaiian luau and the famed big barbecues of our own southwest. There is much we can adapt from the cooking of the ancient Indians.

With the coming of the Europeans, notably the Spanish and the Portuguese, new foods entered the daily diet. The Spanish brought beef, lambs, pigs, goats and chickens. And the Indians adopted them and quickly learned to husband them, until a hundred head of cattle soon became a thousand, to populate the Argentine grasslands. A handful of horses, abandoned during some of the interminable battles for conquest were left to roam the pampas and became great herds of wild horses in a very short time.

It is difficult to imagine how quickly the

interchange of foodstuffs was affected between the Old World and the New. Who can think of Italian cooking without tomatoes? Yet, tomatoes were actually unknown in Europe until the first explorers brought them back in the fifteenth and sixteenth centuries. Potatoes, too, that great staple of Central Europe, had their origins in South America. Conversely, it is hard to imagine the Argentine without cattle. Spices, too, became an important exchange. The Indians had learned to use the marvellous spices – the peppers, the herbs and the barks – in a way hitherto unknown to the Europeans, and they found the subtle blendings a great delight to their palates. (Cinnamon is the secret ingredient of many a South American specialty.) The development of spices became a highly profitable part of the whole European-Latin American trade system and remains so today.

We have mentioned that the Indians in the

mountain countries had perfected a unique system of freeze-drying. They would take potatoes, for example, to the high mountains where the dry, freezing temperatures would quite literally "freeze-dry" them for future use. Preserving in spices was also common. And when the Spanish added onions and garlic to the Indian foodlore, many new ways of preparing and preserving food came into everyday use.

One of the greatest additions to the basic Indian diet was that of fats and dairy products. With fat, it was now possible to fry. Though the ancient methods still dominate most Latin cooking, fats broadened not only the diet, but methods of cooking as well.

When the Portuguese brought slaves from Africa, a new note was added to the cuisines. The Africans, finding the temperature and climate of Brazil much like their own, quickly brought such things from the old world as palms, which thrived in Brazil, giving oil or "dende" as it is called today. Coconuts, too, became an important factor. But, most important was the African skill in preparing and presenting food in an attractive manner. Since few of the Portuguese women who lived on the big estates to which the blacks were brought knew much at all about cooking, the Africans quickly took charge. There is a saying, still popular in Brazil, "the blacker the cook, the better the cooking", and we find exotic African interpretations of the basic Indian-with-Portuguese cuisine throughout Brazil. In all the best restaurants, black men and women still run the kitchens.

As other Europeans came to explore and conquer the rich New World, the cuisines became even more diverse and cosmopolitan. Thus, we find the French touch in Haiti and parts of the West Indies. The Dutch did much to develop the "Spice Islands"; even the British, not generally known for their interest in cookery, added a bit. In later history, the Germans brought beer; the Italians, pasta; vineyards were planted for the development of wines – each country has made its contribution until today, Latin America boasts an amazing amalgam of the cuisines of the world – and offers the North American homemaker a rich source of ideas for brightening her own daily fare. In these times of soaring food costs, it is well to look south of the border for interesting and economical ways to extend the family food budget.

In every village there is a street vendor selling tortillas to be filled with hot and cold stuffings.

Latin American cooking does not require a long list of exotic and expensive spices and foodstuffs. Most of it is based on foods readily available in the great supermarkets all over the United States. The few rare ingredients which might be included in a particular recipe are generally available from a local specialty or gourmet shop. And as interest in Latin American cooking increases, more and more of the basics appear on our market shelves. The huge number of North Americans who visit Mexico each year have brought back such an interest in the somewhat fiery Mexican cooking,

that several stores now carry a complete line of Mexican chiles, pepper, "moles" (sauces). Tortillas are readily available in cans or from the deep freeze.

It is interesting to note, that as one travels through Latin America, the native cooking still relies heavily on the ancient techniques and uses the most readily available foods. From the centuries of invasions, attempted conquests and trades, the Latin Americans have taken only those foods and techniques which were readily assimilated into their own basic culture. They have borrowed heavily of those things

Children carry water from the communal well in a village of Mexico

A tourist stops to buy a small gift from the children in Mexico.

which augment their own requirements and assimilate them well. But note well, that the most successful recipes are not just duplicates of old-country ones, but adaptations to the native custom – we might say they have taken the old cuisines "with a pinch of salt."

In following these recipes, the same principle may apply. Use your imagination if the local market cannot supply you with a particular ingredient. And don't hesitate to use the "convenience" foods, if they suit your needs better. Ground onions and garlic, while not quite so sweet as fresh, are much

simpler to use – and chili sauce in bottles may be sharpened with the addition of a little more chili, or a dash of hot sauce, to simulate the much more time consuming preparation of sauces of the native countries. Have you ever considered basting pork with peanut butter, thinned with a little milk? Or using a big, Halloween-type pumpkin, seeded and buttered, then slowly baked whole as the container (and gravy thickener) for a stew? Explore and discover the little touches and techniques, so typically Latin American, which you can easily adapt to your own table.

In Dutch Guyana, housewives bargain over the price of bananas, plantains, fruit and vegetables.

Exotic fruits fill the streets with fresh sweetness and color.

Geography, quite naturally, has an enormous influence on the cuisine of any country. And since much of the populated portion of Latin America lies in the warm areas, eating habits have been heavily influenced by climate, as well. Add to this the dominance of conquerors from the Mediterranean areas of Europe and a pattern of eating emerges which incorporates the "siesta" hours of Spain with the big appetites of the agrarian workers and places food, its preparation and consumption, as an extremely important factor in the lifestyle of all Latin Americans.

At high altitudes, the boiling point of liquids is lower, so food never seems as hot as it does at sea-level. In the coastal areas, there is a dominance of sea food – marvellous fresh fish, succulent crustaceans – all prepared in a dozen tantalizing ways. From the lush tropic jungles come fruits – in number far beyond the dozen or so of our local markets. (Many even have names for which we have no translation.) And in the rolling grasslands country, there is meat.

Meat is served at nearly every meal. But the meat is not the force-fattened prime beef of our stockyards, so the ways of cooking the somewhat tougher, less rich cuts are many and varied. Each area in Latin America, therefore, has developed singular dishes and ways to present its food. Wherever you go, food is offered. It is a mark of the instinctive Latin hospitality, an item of major importance in Latin life. And it is always presented with color, charm and graciousness.

Dining out in Mexico is a treat when the scenery is so beautiful.

MEXICO

The day begins in Mexico with a cup of chocolate, (Mexican chocolate contains cinnamon, and the flavor is delightful), or a "café con leche" – which is mostly hot milk to which an infusion of coffee is added. Breakfast comes a little later – with fruit, meat and, as at every meal, beans. A "little minute" at eleven or so is taken for a light refreshment, then dinner at two o'clock. This will be several courses: soup, rice, fish, meat, beans, fruit and dessert. Then the long siesta, followed by "merienda" – a hot sweet drink and perhaps a pastry. Later in the evening, about ten, supper, which is much like dinner, but lighter, is served.

Families from Mexico City get together to enjoy a riverboat picnic on the floating gardens of Xochinilco.

Much Mexican cooking is based on the ancient Indian cooking of the Aztecs – with some modern innovations. The "tortilla", a flat pancake of unleavened corn or wheat flour, is the bread of the people. It can also be used as plate, spoon, snack, sandwich, and is the base for many, many dishes throughout the country. To the tortillas in the form of taco, tostada, enchilada, quesadilla or whichever way the cook has decided to use them today, one must add beans as the staple of the Mexican diet. And, inevitably, there are chili peppers in degrees of hotness and sweetness which defy definition. Soups, stews and sweets are the other important ingredients of daily fare. In the coastal areas one finds beautiful fish and abundant tropical fruit. With the advent of air freight, these appear daily in the major markets of Mexico City, too. Whatever the meal, whatever the season, every meal in Mexico is served with color and music – and whenever possible – with good company to add to its enjoyment.

Shoppers stroll through the street markets in Mexico.

14

A beautiful array of fresh, ripe melons

In Mexico, food is omnipresent. Small boys and old women walk the streets of the big cities and of the pueblos with trays laden with sweets for sale. Sidewalk cafés beckon constantly to the passerby to stop for a minute for a coffee, a cup of chocolate, a sip of tequila. In the plazas of Mexico City, old ladies spread their skirts on the ground and make beautiful arrangements of beautiful fresh peaches – great ripe melons – whatever is in season. And the morning markets are a painter's dream of form and color – overlaid with the music of bargaining voices – and guitars.

16

SOUTH AMERICA

The great Inca Empire, which included much of present-day Peru, Ecuador, a large part of Chile and Bolivia and the northwestern part of Argentina, had a tremendous influence on the cooking of those countries, which is still evident today. Potatoes are the diet staple – but potatoes prepared in a variety of ways almost unknown in the United States. Sometimes they are cooked with "aji" – a kind of hot pepper and herbs and spices; often they are swathed in a rich cream or cheese sauce and for special occasions they are molded with cheese, eggs, olives, prawns or corn. In the mountains, the "pachamanca" is a gaudy barbecue; on the coastal areas, charcoal cookery replaces the earth oven. "Antichucos" are the great street food – morsels of beef barbecued on a skewer. Fish dishes are common. "Ceviche" is a tender white fish marinated in spices and citrus, similar to the "poisson crud" of Tahiti.

A Venezuelan shop window displays a dazzling array of dried fish.
The chef knows how succulent the pork will be as carves the meat from a smiling piglet.

Prawns are popular. Peanuts and bananas are vital in northern Peru and Ecuador.

BRAZIL

Most Brazilian dishes are Portuguese in origin. Not so much because the Portuguese were the first non-aboriginal cooks in the country, but because the Portuguese trade controls were so strict that only Portuguese products were added to the already abundant native diet. The Africans imported to work on the big plantations contributed their own magic, and the Germans who settled the Southern states, the Italians and the French who followed have all left their touch on the Brazilian cuisine. But the most impressive thing about eating in Brazil is the prodigality of food. Not only is food plentiful, but the Brazilians would think it a poor meal indeed which did not include visitors to add to their own large and extended families.

Food is as readily available as guests and a meal in Brazil is a great party-like

affair – every day. Meats, often in various forms of preserve and pickle are a staple. So is fruit – oranges, bananas, mangos, papayas, breadfruit and other exotic fruits abound. Coconut is used in many ways. And everywhere there are beans. Black beans are like daily bread – and are even an essential part of the great national fiesta dish, "feijoada completa" which combines them with many smoked and cured meats and garnishes them with fresh fruit. Pumpkins, squashes, okras are all prepared with great imagination and offer many thoughtful suggestions to the North American cook. Farina is the white, toasted meal of manioc and appears on the table alongside the salt and sugar, to be sprinkled on everything. Flowers play a very important part in the social and domestic life of Brazil and blossoms are used freely to decorate dishes at table.

ARGENTINA

In the southern country of Argentina, food, especially meat, is plentiful. The rich, rolling pampas of the Rio de la Plata river provides the people with a year round basket of plenty. Argentinian beef is famous all over the world – and it is said that in olden times the gauchos ate nothing else.

"Empañadas", the tiny meat pies so popular in Spain, here take on a delightful, spicy character and are eaten at all hours of the day. To accompany meat dishes, from the simplest broiled meats to the more colorful and elaborate "matambres" and stews, a side dish made of cornmeal, highly seasoned with onions, garlic, peppers, cinnamon and such is served. Sometimes it is wrapped in corn husks and steamed as with the Mexican tamale, then it is known as "humitas."

The favorite Argentine way to celebrate almost any occasion is with a great "asado", literally, roast. This is really a noisy, gala barbecue – with many kinds of meat, spitted and cooked by a huge open fire or over a "parilla" (grill). The meats are basted with a variety of sauces and the guests constantly comment on the ability of the host to prepare them to succulent perfection.

CHILE

Chile, unlike Argentina, has no vast supply of beef, so fish becomes the favorite source of protein, with beans the everyday "bread." "Porotos granados", highly spiced beans are the national dish. Corn is also an essential part of everyday meals. A recipe for "pastel de cholo" (corn pie) is a family treasure in every household. But the best fare in Chile comes from the sea – and is generally served with colorful sauces and side dishes.

THE CARIBBEAN

The countries of the northern Andes and the Caribbean coast have mastered the fruits which are so plentiful in the great tropical forests. Plantains, a kind of banana, are cooked in every form from stews to sweets. Avocados, too, appear in chunks and slices to enrich stews, as well as in appetizers and sauces. Cornmeal is still the staple and "hallas" are very like the Mexican tamale. An envelope of cornmeal is

Wherever there is food, there is always a small crowd to buy it, sell it or simply to eat it.

filled with most any combination of foodstuffs the cook has on hand, all brightly seasoned, wrapped in a banana leaf then steamed to succulent tenderness. Since much of the beef is mountain-fed and somewhat tough, many ingenious ways have been developed to serve it. Roasts are larded with fat or bacon then stuffed with vegetables and simmered before roasting. Coconuts are in everyday use – the oil for frying, the meat dropped in stews and the milk mixed with sugar for numerous "dulces."

The Caribbean islands tend to reflect the cuisine of the conquering country – but simmered to a "creole" presentation in every life. Many of the Dutch dishes from the islands combine the basic, rather heavy Dutch foods with native spices which add the lightness and fire of a festival. French skills appear in Haiti and Trinidad. And everywhere there is fish and fruit, prepared with special care.

A gaucho watches carefully over an assortment of meats roasting for an asado, the classic Argentinian feast.

CHILE

About 150 miles due west of Mendoza, Argentina, are found Chile's best vineyards. Wine is grown in two thirds of Chile, in areas which vary radically in climate – from very dry in the north to very wet in the south. However, in the middle area around Santiago, the conditions are just right and it is in these vineyards that the best wine is produced. Some of the poorer northern wine is distilled into "Pisco".

VENEZUELA

The drinks most popular in Venezuela are rum, cocuy, cream punch and Creme de Cacao. Cocuy is enjoyed by the poorer people, particularly in the interior and is distilled from the roots of sisal. Ponche Crema (cream punch) has a base of eggs and rum and is made from a secret and very ancient formula. Creme de Cacao is a very sweet liqueur with a strong cocoa-vanilla flavor. The Chouao, which usually figures on Creme de Cacao labels, is that of a district in Venezuela reputed to produce the best cocoa beans in the world.

ARGENTINA

The world's third largest wine producer, Argentina boasts the largest blending vat found anywhere in the world. Most Argentinian wine comes from the state of Mendoza where the climate is arid. The flat, expansive vineyards are irrigated by canals and the vines yield transplanted European grapes brought by Italian immigrants centuries ago.

A good part of the wine remains in Argentina as part of the daily diet, but some is exported. It is ordinary wine but good enough to compare with some of the better Spanish table wines. Rio Negro, a cooler area to the south, is said to make the best wines.

Mexico is famous for its exotic punches and long refreshing coolers.

MEXICO

The selection of drinks varies considerably all over Mexico. The poorer people tend to drink beer and pulque which is a strong liquor made from cactus and, if fermented, can be very potent indeed.

They also drink Tequila which is distilled from the Century Plant, a type of cactus. When Tequila is drunk as an aperitif, one usually follows this procedure: one sip of pure Tequila, one of "Sangrita" (a tomato sauce mixed with Tabasco sauce), one squeeze of lemon juice directly into the mouth, and to finish off, a pinch of salt. This ritual is followed until the glass of Tequila is finished.

Kahlua is Mexico's coffee liqueur and is served with coffee as well as with deserts such as ice cream.

THE CARIBBEAN

Rum-making has been a tradition in all of the Caribbean islands dating back to the 16th century when sugar cane was imported by the Spaniards from Europe (originally from China). Rum is made either by crushing the sugar cane into juice, or from molasses which results from boiling the juice to make sugar. The substance is then fermented and distilled.

Each island uses its own method of flavoring with a variety of tropical fruits or spices to impart a distinctive and individual taste to its brand of rum. Color varies from white through amber, pale gold to dark.

Tia Maria is a liqueur made from Jamaica's famous Blue Mountain coffee. Curaçao is a sweet digestive liqueur made with wine or grape spirit, sugar and orange peel. It was first made by the Dutch using a bitter orange first discovered in Curaçao, a Dutch West Indian island. Triple Sec is the name given to a white Curaçao and originally meant thrice distilled and very dry.

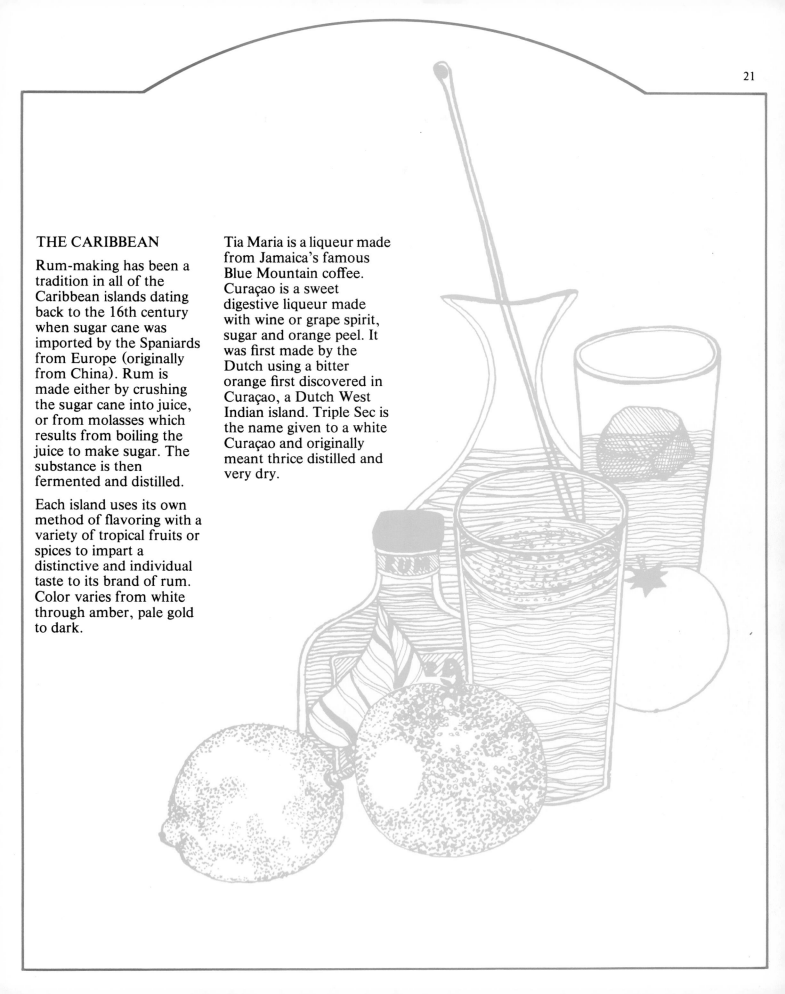

Appetizers

Avocado with shrimp

Abacate com camarão

4 servings

> 1 cup cooked shrimp
> 2 teaspoons lemon juice
> 1 cup diced celery
> 1 hard boiled egg, diced
> ½ teaspoon salt
>   Freshly ground black pepper
> ¼ cup mayonnaise
> 4 avocados

Sprinkle the shrimp with ½ of the lemon juice. Add the celery, egg, salt and pepper and mix with the mayonnaise. Cut the avocados in half and remove the seeds. Sprinkle the cut surface with the remaining lemon juice to prevent discoloration. Fill the avocado halves with the shrimp mixture and chill before serving.

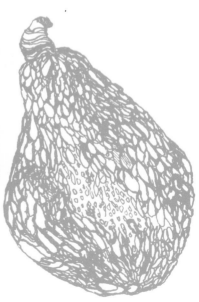

Mexicans prefer interesting combinations of foods to plain meats. Here, beef is thinly sliced, then stuffed with a vegetable sauce for a delicious appetizer.

Stuffed roast beef rolls

Flores de carne

4 servings

  1 cup peeled and chopped
    zucchini, cooked
  1 avocado, peeled, seeded and
    cut into pieces
  1 tablespoon minced onion
  ½ teaspoon chili powder
  2 tablespoons oil
  2 tablespoons vinegar
  ¼ teaspoon salt
 16 slices roast beef
    Lettuce leaves
  3 hard boiled eggs
  8 radishes

Mash the zucchini and avocado until smooth. Combine with the onion, chili powder, oil, vinegar and salt. Place a tablespoon of this sauce on each slice of roast beef. Roll up the beef and tie each roll with string. Cover a serving dish with lettuce leaves and arrange the rolls of beef in a circle as if they were spokes in a wheel. Cut the eggs in half lengthwise. Remove the yolks and force through a strainer. Spoon the strained yolks into the center of the dish. Cut the egg whites into long thin strips and place on the roast beef rolls. Garnish with radish "roses" and serve the remaining sauce separately. Remove string before serving.

24

Egg and spinach hors d'oeuvres

Torta pascualina

8 servings

- ½ pound (12) filo leaves
- 8 tablespoons butter, melted
- 6 tablespoons grated Parmesan cheese
- 2 cups cooked spinach, squeezed dry
- ½ teaspoon salt
  Freshly ground black pepper
- ¼ teaspoon nutmeg
- ¼ cup cream
- 1 tablespoon flour
- 6 hard boiled eggs, sliced

Brush a 9 × 12 × 2 inch baking pan with butter. Cover with 3 layers filo dough, brushing the surface of each layer with melted butter. Sprinkle 1 tablespoon grated cheese over the third layer. Cover with 3 more layers, brushing each layer with butter. Combine 4 tablespoons grated cheese, with the spinach, salt, pepper, nutmeg, cream and flour and mix well. Spread over the layered dough and cover with the egg slices. Repeat the procedure with the remaining 6 leaves of dough, brushing the top layer generously with melted butter. Bake in a preheated 350° oven for 50 minutes until crisp, flaky and golden. Cut into serving pieces and serve hot or cold.

Delicate pastry enfolds a mixture of eggs and spinach for a delicious hors d'oeuvre in Uruguay

Egg and avocado appetizer

Picante de huevos

6 servings

- 6 hard boiled eggs, chopped
- 2 avocados, chopped
- 1 fresh chili pepper, finely chopped or
  ¼ teaspoon chili powder
- 1 onion, finely chopped
- 3 tablespoons finely chopped parsley
- 2 tablespoons vinegar
- ½ teaspoon salt

Place all the ingredients in a blender and blend at medium speed until very well combined and fairly smooth. Chill for several hours. Serve with melba toast as an hors d'oeuvre or on lettuce leaves as an appetizer.

Avocado dip

Guacamole para sopear

4 servings

- 2 avocados, peeled and chopped
- 1 tablespoon minced onion
- 1 tablespoon lemon juice
- ½ cup cream cheese, softened
- ½ cup finely chopped celery
- 1 teaspoon chili powder
- ½ teaspoon salt

Place the avocados, onion and lemon juice in an electric blender and blend until smooth. Beat the cream cheese until light and fluffy. Add the avocado mixture and all the remaining ingredients and combine thoroughly. Serve immediately as a dip for tortillas, chips or crackers.

Bean dip

Frijoles para sopear

4 servings

- 1 cup refried beans (recipe page 72)
- 1 cup sour cream
- ½ tablespoon prepared mustard
- ½ teaspoon salt

Mash the beans and combine with the sour cream and mustard. Mix well and add salt to taste. Use as a dip for fried tortillas, celery sticks or cauliflower.

Egg and spinach hors d'oeuvres

Banana omelette

Tortilla de banana

4 servings

    3 tablespoons butter
    4 bananas, sliced
    6 eggs, separated
  ½ teaspoon salt
      Dash of cayenne pepper
  ¼ cup milk
    2 tablespoons finely chopped
       parsley

Melt the butter in a skillet and sauté the bananas about 5 minutes, turning them frequently. Remove from the pan and set aside. Beat the egg yolks with the salt, cayenne pepper and milk. Beat the egg whites until stiff and fold the yolks and whites together. Transfer to a buttered 7 × 10 inch shallow casserole and arrange the banana slices on top. Bake in a 350° oven 20 minutes until lightly browned. Sprinkle with parsley and serve from the casserole.

Stuffed green peppers

Pimentão com recheio de ovo

4 servings

    4 green peppers, cut in half
       and seeded
    1 cup medium white sauce
       (see below)
    6 hard boiled eggs, finely
       chopped
  ½ cup crumbled fried bacon
    1 teaspoon prepared (Dijon
       type) mustard
  ½ cup fine dry breadcrumbs
    2 tablespoons butter, melted

White sauce:
    2 tablespoons butter
    2 tablespoons flour
  ¼ teaspoon salt
      Freshly ground black pepper
    1 cup milk

To prepare the sauce, melt the butter and stir in the flour. Cook over low heat for 1 minute. Add the seasonings and milk and continue cooking over moderate heat for 2 minutes until the sauce has thickened. Cook the green peppers in boiling salted water for 5 minutes. Drain. Combine the white sauce with the eggs, bacon and mustard. Fill the pepper shells with the mixture. Mix the breadcrumbs and melted butter and top the stuffed peppers with the buttered crumbs. Bake in a preheated 350° oven for 20 minutes.

Jumbo shrimp in wine sauce

Camarone endiablado

4 servings

  ⅓ cup dry white wine
  ¼ cup wine vinegar
    1 tablespoon prepared mustard
    2 tablespoons grated fresh
       horseradish
    2 tablespoons catsup
    1 small clove garlic, crushed
  ½ teaspoon salt
  ¼ teaspoon cayenne pepper
  ½ cup oil
  16 to 20 jumbo shrimp, cooked
       and cleaned with tails left
       intact
       Lettuce leaves
       Paprika

Place the wine, vinegar, mustard, horseradish, catsup, garlic, salt, cayenne pepper and oil in an electric blender and blend until smooth. Place the shrimp in a bowl and add the sauce. Cover and refrigerate at least 8 hours. Arrange lettuce leaves in cocktail glasses and add the shrimp. Spoon some of the marinade over the shrimp and sprinkle with paprika.

'Plantains,' the firm banana-like fruit so popular in South America, are folded into an omelette, dusted with parsley and served as a first course or luncheon dish in Colombia.

Banana omelette

Salads

Crab salad

Salada de caranguejo

4 servings

- 1 (7¾ ounce) can crabmeat or 1½ cups fresh crab
- 1 fennel bulb, cleaned and cut into strips (if available)
- 1 cup bean sprouts, cooked
- 1 green pepper, peeled, seeded and cut into thin strips
- 1 red pepper, peeled, seeded and cut into strips
- ¼ teaspoon salt
- ½ teaspoon dry mustard Freshly ground black pepper
- 1 tablespoon lemon juice
- 1 tablespoon wine vinegar
- 6 tablespoons olive oil
- 1 tablespoon soy sauce

Flake the crabmeat into small pieces and mix with the fennel bulb, bean sprouts and peppers. Toss lightly. Combine the salt, mustard, pepper, lemon juice and vinegar until well blended. Add the oil and beat until smooth. Add the soy sauce and mix well. Toss lightly with the salad when ready to serve.

Christmas salad

Ensalada de Noche Buena

4 to 6 servings

- 1 cup diced cooked beets
- 1 cup diced fresh pineapple
- 1 cup diced apple
- ½ cup mandarin oranges (canned)
- ½ cup sliced bananas
- ½ cup peeled and sliced guava
- 2 tablespoons lemon juice
- 6 tablespoons pomegranate seeds (optional)
- 1 cup light cream Sugar

Toss the beets and fruits together lightly in a glass bowl. Sprinkle with lemon juice to prevent discoloring and decorate with pomegranate seeds. Serve with light cream and sugar.

Molded pineapple salad

Salada de ananás

4 to 6 servings

- 1 package lemon flavored gelatin
- 1 cup hot water
- 1 cup cold water Juice of ½ lemon Pinch of salt
- 1 carrot, peeled and grated
- 1 (8 ounce) can crushed pineapple, thoroughly drained

Place the gelatin in a mixing bowl. Add the hot water and stir until the gelatin is dissolved. Add the remaining ingredients and transfer to a ring mold which has been rinsed in cold water. Refrigerate 2 to 3 hours until firm. Unmold on a serving plate.

Peasant salad

Ensalata campesina

6 servings

- 1 cup dried chick peas or 2 cups canned, drained chick peas
- ½ pound cream cheese, diced
- 2 onions, thinly sliced
- ½ cup olive oil
- ¼ cup lemon juice
- 1 teaspoon salt
- ½ teaspoon coriander
- 3 hard boiled eggs, quartered

Soak the dried chick peas overnight in water to cover. Drain, add fresh water and cook for 1½ hours or until tender. (If canned chick peas are used, omit these steps.) Drain and chill for 2 hours. Combine the chick peas, cheese and onions in a bowl. Mix the olive oil, lemon juice, salt and coriander together. Pour over the chick pea mixture and toss lightly. Serve, well chilled, on lettuce leaves. Garnish with hard boiled eggs.

'Ensalada de Noche Buena' – the Christmas salad of Mexico, combines the richness of apples, oranges and bananas with a sweetened dressing and cubes of beets and pomegranate seeds for color.

Chicken and corn salad

Bocado primavera de ave

6 servings

3 cups diced cooked chicken
2 cups canned corn, drained
6 tomatoes, peeled, seeded
  and chopped
3 green peppers, seeded and
  chopped
2 cups mayonnaise
½ teaspoon salt
  Freshly ground black pepper
6 lettuce leaves
3 hard boiled eggs, quartered

Place the chicken, corn,
tomatoes, green peppers, 1 cup
mayonnaise, salt and pepper in
a bowl and combine gently but
thoroughly. Arrange the lettuce
leaves on individual serving
plates and heap the salad on the
leaves in smooth mounds. Coat
the salad completely with the
remaining mayonnaise and
garnish with the eggs. Chill at
least 1 hour before serving.

*Chicken and corn – two basic
elements in South American
cooking – are combined in a hearty
salad from Chile.*

Stuffed cucumber salad

Salada de pepino recheado

4 servings

    4 (8 inch) cucumbers
    ¾ teaspoon salt
    4 (3 ounce) packages cream
       cheese
    2 tablespoons grated onion
    3 tablespoons finely chopped
       green and red pepper
    1 teaspoon paprika
       Freshly ground black pepper
       Lettuce leaves
    2 tomatoes, peeled, seeded and
       quartered
       Mayonnaise

Cut off the ends of the
cucumbers and score the skin
lengthwise with the tines of a
fork. Halve the cucumbers
crosswise and remove the seedy
centers with an apple corer.
Sprinkle the insides with ½
teaspoon salt and place on a
rack to drain. Meanwhile,
combine the cream cheese,
onion, green pepper, paprika,
remaining salt and pepper and
stuff the cucumbers with the
mixture. Wrap each piece in
aluminum foil and refrigerate
overnight. When ready to serve,
slice the stuffed cucumbers and
arrange on a bed of lettuce
leaves. Garnish with tomatoes
and a little mayonnaise.

*Brazilian salads are colorful and
cool. Cucumbers are stuffed, then
sliced and served on a bed of
greens with a garnish of tomato
wedges.*

Mixed salad

Ensalada de guacamole

4 servings

    1 ripe avocado, peeled, seeded
       and cut into pieces
    1 large tomato, peeled, seeded
       and chopped
    1 tablespoon finely chopped
       onion
    3 tablespoons vinegar
    3 tablespoons oil
    ¼ teaspoon chili powder
    ¼ teaspoon salt
    1 cup Mexican beans or kidney
       beans, cooked
    1 cup green beans, cooked
    4 stalks celery, chopped
    1 head lettuce, shredded

Place the first 7 ingredients in an
electric blender. Blend to form a
smooth purée. Pour this sauce
over a mixed salad, made with
the remaining ingredients.

Stuffed cucumber salad

Chilean salad

Salpicon

4 servings

    2 cups diced cold cooked veal,
       lamb or chicken
    1 teaspoon onion juice
    6 mint leaves, chopped or
       ½ teaspoon dried mint
    1 head Boston lettuce, shredded
    2 tablespoons finely chopped
       parsley
    ¼ cup French dressing
    2 hard boiled eggs, sliced

Place the meat, onion juice,
mint, lettuce and parsley in a
salad bowl. Add the French
dressing and toss the salad until
the ingredients are thoroughly
combined. Serve on crisp lettuce
leaves and garnish with sliced
eggs.

Cabbage salad

Salada de salmagundi

6 servings

    1 package unflavored gelatin
    ¼ cup water
    1½ cups tomato juice
    1 bay leaf
    1 whole clove
    3 peppercorns
    ¼ cup sugar
    ½ teaspoon salt
    ¼ cup vinegar
    1 teaspoon onion juice
    ½ cup shredded cabbage
    1 cup finely chopped celery
    1 canned pimiento, cut into
       strips
    2 tablespoons chopped red or
       green pepper

Sprinkle the gelatin over the
water to soften. Place the tomato
juice, bay leaf, clove and
peppercorns in a saucepan and
bring to a boil. Lower the heat
and simmer 5 minutes. Strain
the liquid into a bowl. Add the
softened gelatin, sugar and salt
and stir until dissolved. Stir in
the vinegar and onion juice and
let the mixture cool. When it
begins to thicken, fold in the
cabbage, celery, pimiento and
green pepper. Place the salad in
a mold which has been rinsed
with cold water. Refrigerate 2 to
3 hours until set. Unmold on a
serving plate.

In Latin America, nearly every meal begins with soup. But soups are not just simple catch-alls of meat and vegetables. The Latin Americans create soups of great distinction with subtle blends of spice and seasoning.
Furthermore, the title, 'sopa', does not necessarily mean that the dish will be mainly liquid. In Mexico, especially, 'dry soups' (sopa seca) are commonly served. These are recipes where the liquid is completely absorbed by the rice or vermicelli cooked in the stock. Other recipes are prepared, then the liquid is poured off to be served in a cup and the solids are sliced and arranged on a platter.
Meat and fowl are the mainstay of the stock bases throughout Latin America, but it would be difficult to find more delicious fish stews and soups than along the coasts and in the islands.
Beans and lentils are often used to make a hearty soup. Potatoes, too, are in common usage. But uncommon additions such as chunks of squash or pumpkin; slices of rich green avocado, grated or chunked coconut add the really unusual and exotic touch which is typically Latin American. Fruit soups, too, are very popular. And always, the ingredients in the soup are served with a very special eye for color and appetite appeal. Sometimes a fresh blossom is floated on the dish, or a bit of fern is used for garnish. Hard boiled eggs, sliced or seived; a dainty lemon slice – or perhaps a curl of orange rind may be added.
With these small touches, the humble soup becomes a festive party dish whenever it is served.

Chicken soup—see recipe page 30

The famous 'canja,' a rich chicken soup from Brazil, conjures up all the magic of its African, Portuguese and South American origins.

Chicken soup

Canja

4 to 6 servings

- 3 tablespoons butter
- 1 onion, finely chopped
- 1 (2½ pound) chicken, cut into serving pieces
- 6 cups water
- 1 sprig parsley
- 2 carrots, sliced
- 1 leek, sliced
- 1 tablespoon finely chopped chives
- 1 teaspoon salt
  Freshly ground black pepper
- 1 cup rice

Heat the butter in a large saucepan and sauté the onion until softened. Add the chicken pieces and sauté until lightly browned on all sides. Add the water, parsley, carrots, leek, chives, salt and pepper and bring to a boil. Lower the heat, cover and simmer 35 to 40 minutes until the chicken is tender. Strain the broth into a clean saucepan and skim off the fat. Reserve vegetables. Remove the skin and bones of the chicken and cut the meat into 2 inch pieces. Bring the broth to a boil. Add the rice and stir once with a fork. Lower the heat, cover and simmer 20 minutes. Add chicken meat and vegetables and cook 5 minutes more.

Chicken soup with vegetables

Sancochi di galinja

6 servings

- 8 cups water
- 2 teaspoons salt
- 1 (2 to 3 pound) chicken, cut into serving pieces
- 1 pound beef marrow bones
- 2 onions, sliced into rings
- 2 leeks, sliced into rings
- 8 sprigs celery leaves
- 3 potatoes, peeled and cubed
- 2 sweet potatoes, peeled and cubed
- ½ cup corn
- 1 green pepper, seeded and cubed
- ¾ pound pumpkin, peeled and cubed
  Freshly ground black pepper

Bring the water and salt to a boil in a large saucepan. Add the chicken and beef bones. Lower the heat, cover and simmer 2 hours. Strain the broth into a clean saucepan. Discard the skin and bones of the chicken and the beef bones. Cut the chicken meat into small pieces. Add the remaining ingredients to the broth. Cover and simmer 30 minutes. Add the chicken meat and simmer 5 minutes more. Taste for seasoning and serve.

Watercress soup

Sopa de agrião

6 to 8 servings

- 2 tablespoons butter
- 1 onion, chopped
- 2 large potatoes, peeled and cubed
- 1 carrot, sliced
- 8 cups chicken broth
- ½ teaspoon salt
  Freshly ground black pepper
- 1 bunch watercress, washed and trimmed
- 2 cups boiling water
- 6 tablespoons heavy cream

Melt the butter in a large saucepan and sauté the onion until transparent. Add the potatoes, carrot, broth, salt and pepper and bring to a boil. Lower the heat, cover and simmer 20 minutes until potatoes and carrot are tender. Meanwhile, cook the watercress in the boiling water 5 minutes. Drain and place in the jar of a blender. Add the soup and blend until smooth. You will have to do this in 2 batches. Return the soup to the saucepan and heat until just simmering. Serve immediately with a tablespoon of cream in the center of each serving.

Potato soup

Ajiaco

6 servings

- 4 tablespoons butter
- 3 onions, finely chopped
- 2 tablespoons flour
- 3 cups chicken broth
- 4 potatoes, peeled and diced
- ⅛ teaspoon saffron
- 1½ teaspoons salt
- ⅛ teaspoon cayenne pepper
- 3 cups milk
- ½ cup green peas
- 3 eggs
- ¼ pound cream cheese
- 1 avocado, peeled and sliced

Heat the butter in a large saucepan. Add the onions and fry for 10 minutes. Add the flour and mix until smooth. Add the chicken broth gradually, stirring constantly until boiling. Add the potatoes, saffron, salt and cayenne pepper and simmer for 20 minutes. Add the milk and peas and continue cooking gently for 5 minutes. Beat the eggs and cream cheese together in a bowl and gradually add 2 cups of the hot soup, beating constantly to avoid curdling. Return the contents of the bowl to the saucepan and heat but do not boil. Place a few thin slices of avocado in each soup plate and pour the hot soup over them.

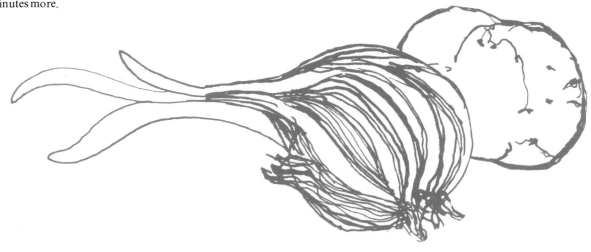

Green pea soup

Sopa de chicharo

4 servings

   3 *cups fresh green peas*
   4 *cups water*
   ½ *onion, chopped*
   1 *clove garlic, crushed*
   3 *tablespoons butter*
   3 *tablespoons flour*
   1 *teaspoon salt*
   ¼ *teaspoon chili powder*
   ½ *cup canned corn*
   ½ *cup warm cream*
   3 *tablespoons finely chopped*
      fresh coriander or parsley

Combine the peas, water, onion and garlic in a saucepan. Bring to a boil and simmer for 10 minutes until tender. Drain and force through a strainer to form a purée. Heat the butter in a saucepan. Stir in the flour and add the purée gradually, stirring constantly. Add the salt, chili powder, corn and cream. Heat thoroughly and sprinkle with coriander or parsley before serving.

Tortilla soup

Sopa de tortilla

4 servings

   4 *slices lean bacon, chopped*
   1 *onion, finely chopped*
   ½ *canned green serrano chili,*
      minced
   8 *tortillas (recipe page 37)*
      cut into strips
   4 *cups beef broth*
   ½ *teaspoon salt*
   ½ *cup grated cheddar cheese*

Fry the bacon in a saucepan until the fat has rendered. Add the onion and chili and sauté 5 minutes. Add the tortilla strips and sauté 3 minutes more. Add the broth and salt and bring to a boil. Ladle the soup into individual ovenproof bowls. Sprinkle with cheese and bake in a 475° oven 5 minutes or until the cheese has formed a golden brown crust.

Green corn soup

Sopa de milho verde

4 servings

   3 *cups canned or frozen corn*
   ½ *cup milk*
   ½ *cup chopped scallions*
   4 *cups chicken broth*
   4 *tablespoons chopped parsley*
   4 *tablespoons butter*
   2 *tablespoons flour*
   1 *teaspoon salt*
      Freshly ground black pepper

Combine the corn, milk and scallions in an electric blender and blend to a smooth purée. Heat the chicken broth, add the corn purée and parsley and cook for 15 minutes. Heat the butter, stir in the flour and gradually add the corn mixture, stirring constantly. Season with salt and pepper. Cook for 5 minutes and serve hot.

Avocado soup

Sopa de aguacate

4 to 6 servings

   2 *large avocados, cut into*
      small pieces
   ½ *teaspoon salt*
      Pinch of white pepper
   1 *cup heavy cream*
   4 *cups chicken broth*
   ⅓ *cup dry sherry*
   1 *small avocado, thinly sliced*

Place the large avocados, salt, pepper and ½ cup cream in the jar of a blender and blend until smooth. Add the remaining cream and blend just until combined. Heat the broth to boiling point and stir in the avocado purée. Add the sherry and sliced avocado, taste for seasoning and remove from the heat. The soup may be served hot or cold.

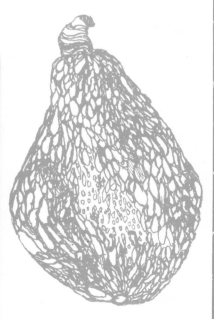

Rich green avocado is cooked in a creamy chicken broth – served hot or cold in Mexico as 'sopa de aguacate.'

Avocado soup

Black bean soup

Sopa de caroatas negras

6 servings

- 1 cup black beans, soaked overnight and drained
  Water
- 2 tablespoons oil
- 1 leek, sliced into rings
- 1 onion, finely chopped
- 1 clove garlic, crushed
- 6 cups beef broth
- ½ teaspoon salt
- 1 tablespoon brown sugar
- 2 tablespoons butter
- 1 cup toasted bread strips

Place the beans in a large saucepan and add water to cover by 1 inch. Bring to a boil, lower the heat and simmer, covered, 2 to 3 hours until the beans are tender. Heat the oil in another large saucepan and sauté the leek, onion and garlic until golden brown. Add the broth, salt and sugar and simmer 10 minutes. Drain the excess water from the beans and add the beans to the broth. Stir in the butter and simmer 2 minutes. Add the bread strips to the soup and serve immediately.

Hearty soups, flavorful and nutritious are staples in Venezuela. Here, black beans simmer with leeks and onions for a filling, flavorful dish

Bean soup

Sopa frijoles

4 servings

- 1 cup frijoles (Mexican beans) or kidney beans
- 4 cups water
- 1 onion, sliced
- 1 clove garlic, crushed
- 1½ teaspoons chili powder
- 1 teaspoon salt
- 6 tablespoons Mozzarella, Muenster or goat cheese, cut into small pieces
- 1 cup fried croutons

Soak the beans in water overnight. Drain. Bring 4 cups water to a boil, add the beans and cook gently for 2½ to 3 hours until the beans are tender. Add the onion, garlic, chili powder and salt and cook for 10 minutes. Force the soup through a strainer or purée in an electric blender. Add water if necessary to make a thick soup. Serve the soup in individual bowls, and garnish with cheese and croutons.

Spinach soup with shrimp

Callalu

6 servings

- 2 pounds spinach, washed and trimmed
- 1 onion, chopped
- ½ pound smoked ham
- 6 cups water
- 12 okra, stems removed
- 12 shrimp, shelled and deveined
- 12 shallots or scallions, finely chopped
- 1 teaspoon salt
  Freshly ground black pepper
- ¼ teaspoon thyme

Combine the spinach, onion, ham and water in a large saucepan. Bring to a boil, reduce the heat and simmer for 20 minutes. Add the okra, shrimp, shallots, salt, pepper and thyme. Cook for another 20 minutes. Remove the ham and cut into small cubes. Return ham to the soup and serve hot.

Lettuce soup

Crema de alface

4 servings

- 2 tablespoons butter
- 1 small onion, finely chopped
- 1 head Boston lettuce, shredded
- 4 cups chicken broth
- ½ teaspoon salt
  Freshly ground black pepper
- ¼ cup light cream
- 1 egg yolk, lightly beaten

Heat the butter in a saucepan and sauté the onion until softened. Add the lettuce, broth, salt and pepper and bring to a boil. Lower the heat, cover and simmer 30 minutes. Combine the cream and egg yolk in a small bowl and add to the soup, stirring constantly. Remove from the heat and serve immediately.

Black bean soup

Shrimp soup 1

Chupe de camarones 1

8 servings

- 2 tablespoons oil
- 1 medium sized onion, finely chopped
- 3 cloves garlic, crushed
- 1 medium sized tomato, peeled, seeded and chopped
- 2 to 3 canned hot chilies, minced
- 1 teaspoon salt
  Freshly ground black pepper
  Pinch of oregano
- 3 medium sized potatoes, peeled
- ½ pound fresh peas
- ½ cup rice
- 8 cups water
- 16 large shrimp, shelled and deveined
- 1 (12 ounce) can corn, drained
- 3 eggs, lightly beaten
- 1 cup evaporated milk
- 1 tablespoon finely chopped parsley

Heat the oil in a large saucepan. Add the onion and garlic and sauté until softened. Add the tomato, chilies, salt, pepper and oregano and sauté 5 minutes, stirring occasionally. Chop 2 of the potatoes very finely and place in the saucepan. Add the peas, rice and water and bring to a boil. Lower the heat and simmer 15 minutes. Cut the remaining potato into large chunks and add to the soup. Continue simmering 20 minutes until the potato is tender. Add the shrimp and corn and simmer 4 to 5 minutes or until the shrimp turn pink. Do not overcook. Add the eggs and stir for a few minutes until the eggs form strings. Remove from the heat and stir in the evaporated milk and parsley. Serve immediately.

Shrimp soup 2

Chupe de camarones 2

6 to 8 servings

- 2 tablespoons olive oil
- 1 onion, finely chopped
- 2 cloves garlic
- 3 tablespoons tomato sauce
- 6 cups fish broth, or use ½ clam juice and ½ water
- ½ cup green peas
- ½ cup corn
- 2 large potatoes, peeled cubed
- 1 teaspoon salt
- ¼ teaspoon chili powder
- 1 (3 ounce) package cream cheese
- 2 cups milk
- 24 large shrimp, shelled and deveined
- 4 eggs, lightly beaten
- 6 small fillets of fried fish

Heat the oil in a large saucepan and sauté the onion and garlic until nicely browned. Remove and discard the garlic cloves. Add the tomato sauce, fish broth, peas, corn, potatoes, salt, chili powder and marjoram. Bring to a simmer and cook 20 minutes. Beat the cream cheese until soft and add it bit by bit to the soup, stirring constantly. Stir in the milk, bring to a simmer and add the shrimp. Cook 3 minutes and remove from the heat. Gradually add 2 cups of the hot soup to the eggs, stirring constantly. Pour the egg mixture back into the soup and reheat over low heat, stirring constantly. Do not allow the soup to boil or the eggs will curdle. Place a piece of fried fish in each soup bowl, and ladle the soup over the fish.

Peanut soup 1

Sopa de amendoim

8 servings

- 1 (2½ pound) chicken, cut into serving pieces
- 8 cups water
- ½ pound beef, cut into small pieces
- 1 onion, chopped
- 2 tablespoons finely chopped parsley
- 1 tomato, quartered
- 1 carrot, peeled and sliced
- 1½ teaspoons salt
  Freshly ground black pepper
- 1 cup unsalted peanuts
- 1 cup water
- 1 cup fresh green peas
- 1 cup cooked rice
- 4 potatoes, peeled and cubed

Combine the chicken, water, cubed beef, onion, parsley, tomato, carrot, salt and pepper in a large saucepan. Bring to a boil, reduce the heat and simmer for 40 minutes until the chicken and meat are tender. Strain the soup and remove the meat and chicken. Remove the skin and bones from the chicken and cut the chicken into small pieces. Blanch the peanuts to remove the skins. Blend in an electric blender with the water until smooth. Add this mixture to the chicken broth, with the chicken, meat, peas, rice and potatoes. Simmer for 15 minutes. **Note:** The amount of peas and rice depends on how thick you wish the soup to be.

Peanut soup 2

Pinda bravoe

6 servings

- 1 pound stewing beef, cut into 1 inch cubes
- 6 cups water
- 4 beef bouillon cubes
- 1 onion, finely chopped
- ¼ teaspoon salt
  Freshly ground black pepper
- 1 cup peanut butter
- 1 green pepper, seeded and chopped
- 4 canned pimientos, cut into strips

Place the beef, water, bouillon cubes, onion, salt and pepper in a saucepan and bring to a boil. Lower the heat, cover and simmer 2 hours until the beef is tender. Place the peanut butter in a bowl and gradually add 1 cup of the hot broth, stirring until the peanut butter is dissolved. Add the peanut butter mixture back to the soup, a little at a time, stirring constantly. Add the green pepper and simmer, uncovered, 15 minutes. Stir in the pimiento strips and serve.

Sauces

Hot avocado sauce

Guacamole

4 servings

- 2 avocados, peeled and chopped
- 2 large tomatoes, peeled, seeded and chopped
- 2 canned green serrano chilies, minced
- 1 medium sized onion, finely chopped
- ½ teaspoon salt
- 2 tablespoons finely chopped coriander or parsley

Place the avocados and tomatoes in a bowl and mash with the back of a fork. Add all the remaining ingredients and combine thoroughly. Serve immediately with tacos, tortillas or tostados. If you do not plan to serve the sauce immediately, cover tightly with plastic wrap because it darkens when exposed to the air.

Hot red sauce

Salsa ranchero

4 servings

- 2 hot red chilies, seeded and cut into pieces
- 2 cups canned whole tomatoes
- 2 medium sized onions, chopped
- 1 clove garlic
- 1 teaspoon ground coriander
- ½ teaspoon sugar
- ½ teaspoon salt
- 1 tablespoon wine vinegar
- 1 tablespoon chopped parsley

Combine the chilies, tomatoes, onions, garlic, coriander and sugar in an electric blender and blend until smooth. Add salt, vinegar and parsley. Serve hot or cold with chicken, fried eggs, tomatoes or tacos.

Green chili pepper sauce

Salsa verde

4 servings

- 4 large tomatoes, peeled and seeded
- 1 small onion, finely chopped
- 2 tablespoons chopped fresh coriander or ½ teaspoon dried coriander
- 1 clove garlic, crushed
- 1 teaspoon chopped green serrano chili (canned)
- ½ teaspoon salt
- Freshly ground black pepper

Combine all the ingredients in an electric blender and blend to form a smooth sauce. The green sauce can be served hot or cold. It is traditionally used as a sauce for meat, tacos, tostados and enchiladas.

Green pea sauce

Salsa de chícaro

4 to 6 servings

- 1 cup cooked green peas
- 2 tomatoes, peeled, seeded and chopped
- 3 tablespoons finely chopped onion
- 2 tablespoons vinegar
- 2 tablespoons oil
- 1 tablespoon chopped capers
- 2 tablespoons finely chopped green pepper
- 2 tablespoons chopped green olives
- ¼ teaspoon thyme
- ½ teaspoon salt
- Freshly ground black pepper

Place the peas and tomatoes in a bowl and mash with the back of a fork. Add the onion, vinegar and oil and beat vigorously. Blend in all the remaining ingredients. Serve the sauce with fish, veal or tongue.

Shrimp sauce

Molho de camarão

4 servings

- 4 *tablespoons butter*
- 4 *large shrimp, cut in small pieces*
- ¾ *teaspoon salt*
  Freshly ground black pepper
- 1 *onion, chopped*
- 1 *tablespoon chopped parsley*
- 2 *tomatoes, peeled, seeded and chopped*
- 1 *cup water*
- 1 *tablespoon cornstarch dissolved in*
  2 *tablespoons tomato ketchup*

Heat the butter in a saucepan, add the shrimp and fry for 3 minutes. Add the salt, pepper, onion and parsley and cook until the onion has softened. Add the tomatoes, water and the cornstarch dissolved in the tomato ketchup. Bring to a boil, reduce the heat and simmer, stirring constantly until thickened.

Curry sauce

Molho de curry

4 servings

- 4 *tablespoons butter*
- 1 *onion, finely chopped*
- 2 *tablespoons flour*
- 1 *to 3 teaspoons curry powder, to taste*
- 1 *cup beef broth*
- 1 *apple, peeled and chopped*
- ½ *teaspoon salt*
- 1 *tablespoon apple chutney*
- ½ *teaspoon lemon juice*

Melt the butter in a saucepan. Add the onion and fry for 5 minutes until golden brown. Stir in the flour and curry powder and cook 1 minute. Add the beef broth gradually, stirring constantly, and cook until the sauce is smooth. Add the chopped apple and salt. Cover and simmer for 20 minutes. Stir in the apple chutney and lemon juice and serve hot.

Parsley sauce

Salsa perejil

4 servings

- ½ *cup finely chopped parsley*
- ¼ *cup blanched and chopped almonds*
- 6 *tablespoons olive oil*
- 3 *tablespoons wine vinegar*
- 1 *teaspoon sugar*
- ½ *clove garlic, crushed*
- ½ *teaspoon salt*
  Freshly ground black pepper

Place all the ingredients in the blender. Blend to form a smooth purée. Serve with fish, veal, cooked meat or vegetables such as cauliflower, carrots or tomatoes.

Almond sauce

Salsa de almendras

4 servings

- 2 *tablespoons lard or oil*
- 2 *tablespoons minced onion*
- 1 *small clove garlic, crushed*
- 1 *tablespoon sugar*
- 2 *tablespoons vinegar*
- ¼ *cup tomato sauce*
- ½ *cup finely chopped almonds*
- ¼ *teaspoon salt*
  Freshly ground black pepper

Heat the lard or oil in a saucepan and sauté the onion and garlic until golden brown. Add the sugar, vinegar, tomato sauce and almonds and cook, stirring, 2 minutes. Season with salt and pepper. Serve the sauce hot with fish, chicken or tongue.

Spicy chocolate sauce

Mole poblano

- 10 dried ancho chili peppers
- 2 cups boiling water
- 5 tablespoons dried almonds
- 2 onions, chopped
- 2 cloves garlic, crushed
- 3 tomatoes, peeled, seeded and chopped
- ½ cup raisins
- 1 tortilla (recipe page 37) fried in oil and broken into pieces
- 2 tablespoons sesame seeds
- ½ teaspoon cinnamon
- ½ teaspoon ground cloves
- ½ teaspoon coriander seeds
- ½ teaspoon salt
- 4 tablespoons lard
- 2 cups chicken broth
- 1½ ounces Mexican chocolate, cut into small pieces

Cut the peppers in quarters and soak in boiling water 1 hour. Retain water. Discard the stems and seeds of the peppers and place the peppers in the jar of an electric blender. Add the almonds, onions, garlic, tomatoes, raisins, tortilla, sesame seeds, cinnamon, cloves, coriander, salt and a few tablespoons of the water in which the chili is soaked. Blend at medium speed, adding tablespoons of water if necessary, until a paste is formed. Heat the lard in a saucepan and add the chili paste. Cook, stirring, 2 or 3 minutes. Add the broth gradually, stirring constantly.
Add the chocolate and stir until melted. The sauce should be the consistency of heavy cream. If it seems too thick, add a little of the chili soaking water. This sauce is served with tortillas, tamales, turkey and chicken.

Brazilian barbecue sauce

Molho de churrasco

- 3 cups vinegar
- 1 tablespoon salt
- 1 tablespoon sugar
- 2 cloves garlic, crushed
- 1 small onion, finely chopped
- 2 tablespoons finely chopped parsley
- 8 small chili peppers, chopped
- 1 teaspoon rosemary
- 1 teaspoon basil
- 1 teaspoon thyme
- 1 teaspoon marjoram

Place all the ingredients in a glass jar. Cover and shake vigorously. Store in the refrigerator until ready to use.

Venezuelan barbecue

Guasacaca

- 1 avocado, peeled and chopped
- 2 tomatoes, peeled, seeded and chopped
- 1 cup olive oil
- 3 tablespoons vinegar
- 1 teaspoon prepared mustard
- ½ teaspoon salt
- 1 red pepper, seeded and finely chopped
- 2 onions, finely chopped
- 1 tablespoon finely chopped parsley

Place the avocado and tomatoes in a bowl and mash with a fork until fairly smooth. Combine the remaining ingredients and stir into the avocado/tomato mixture.

Tortillas

Tortillas

Tortillas

20 to 24 Tortillas

*2 cups masa harina
  (corn flour)
1 teaspoon salt
1 to 1¼ cups warm water*

Combine the masa harina and salt in a bowl. Add the warm water gradually, kneading the mixture until it can be gathered into a ball. On humid days, you will need only the minimum amount of water. The dough should not be sticky. Let it rest for 30 minutes. Form pieces of the dough into walnut sized balls. Dust a board and rolling pin very generously with corn flour. Roll the balls out into 5 to 6 inch rounds. If the dough tends to stick, return it to the bowl and knead in a little more flour. If it seems too dry add a few drops of water and knead thoroughly. Rub an 8 to 9 inch cast iron skillet with shortening or lard and heat it over medium heat. Cook the tortillas until dry, about 2 minutes on each side. As they are done, wrap them in foil and keep warm in a very low oven. To serve, wrap them in a linen napkin and place in a basket. If you make the tortillas in advance, reheat them in an ungreased skillet for a few seconds on each side.

Mexican tacos are tortillas stuffed with a hot tomato flavored chicken mixture, rolled and quickly fried to crisp the tortilla. Avocado crescents are added as a cool garnish.

Tortillas

*2 cups flour
1 teaspoon salt
1 teaspoon baking powder
3 tablespoons lard
½ cup water*

Sift the flour, salt and baking powder together into a bowl. Cut the lard into the flour with a pastry blender or 2 knives. Add the water gradually, stirring with a fork. Knead the dough into a ball and set it aside for 30 minutes. Pinch off walnut sized pieces of the dough and roll each piece out on a lightly floured board into a round 6 inches in diameter and ⅛ inch thick. Heat an ungreased cast iron skillet until a drop of water sizzles on the surface. Cook the tortillas about 1 minute on each side until lightly flecked with brown. As the tortillas are done, wrap them in foil and keep warm in a 200° oven.

The 'tortilla' of Mexico is probably the heartiest dish ever devised by man (or, more likely by woman!). It is not only the daily bread of the country, but it is the base of a large number of everyday and festival dishes. It can be crisped and used to hold all sorts of fillings – meat, fish, vegetables. (Then it is called a 'taco'.) It can be fried, filled and sauced and then baked in a dozen different ways as an enchilada. It can be made large or small to suit the particular requirement of the cook. It can be broken up to thicken soups – or toasted to serve with appetizers. In the United States, young people in particular have found it a wonderful addition to the 'snack culture' – and fill it with everything from hamburger (with or without chili sauce) to peanut butter and jelly! The tortilla is most commonly made of 'mais', the corn flour native to Latin America, but it may also be made from wheat or rice flour. Where once it was entirely a hand operation – (and it is quite a sight to watch a skilled woman pat the little ball of dough into measured sizes of flat cakes), tortilla making is now done by machines which knead and roll the dough into a standard form. In most Mexican cities, even the poor buy their daily ration of tortillas from a tiny shop in the square. Tortillas may be both canned or frozen, and a supply on hand makes it easy to turn a simple hamburger into a festive meal. Tamales, and 'hallacas' are essentially envelopes of corn-meal dough filled with meat or vegetables, or sometimes sweetened fruit, then wrapped in either corn husks or banana leaves (though plain parchment will also serve), and steamed until the flavors have blended and cooked through. This kind of preparation makes them excellent choices for picnic meals.

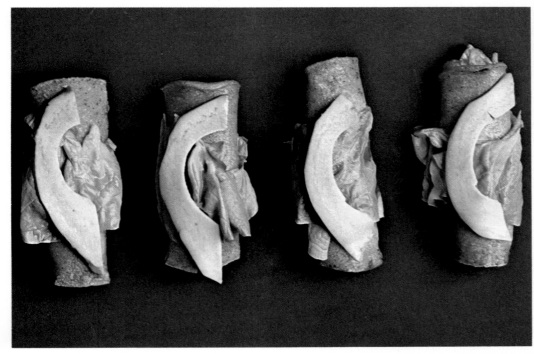

Tacos with chicken—see recipe page 39

Rice pancake

Tortilla de arroz

4 to 6 servings

  2 tablespoons oil
  1 onion, finely chopped
  1 small red pepper, finely
     chopped
  2 cloves garlic, crushed
  1 cup rice
  1 teaspoon salt
  2 cups boiling water
  3 eggs
  ½ cup grated Parmesan cheese

Heat the oil in a saucepan and
sauté the onion, red pepper and
garlic 5 minutes over medium
heat. Add the rice and salt and
cook, stirring, for about
2 minutes until the rice is
opaque. Add the water and stir
once with a fork. Lower the
heat, cover and simmer 25
minutes or until the rice has
absorbed all the liquid. Remove
from the heat and set aside
until the rice is cold. Beat the
eggs with the cheese and
combine with the cold rice.
Transfer to a large shallow
fireproof skillet or baking pan.
Place under the broiler for 5
minutes until the top has
browned. Serve immediately.

Tortillas Gudalajara style

Enchiladas Guadalajara

4 servings

  2 cups diced cooked chicken
     or turkey
  ½ cup chopped black olives
  ½ cup chopped almonds
  2 tablespoons finely chopped
     onion
  1 cup green chili pepper
     sauce (recipe page 34)
 12 tortillas (recipe page 37)
  ½ cup grated Parmesan cheese
  2 tablespoons butter

In a bowl, combine the chicken,
olives, almonds and onion.
Heat the chili sauce and spread
each tortilla with a little of the
sauce. Spread a portion of the
chicken mixture over the sauce
and roll up the tortillas. Place
them in a shallow buttered
baking dish and spoon the
remaining chili sauce on top.
Sprinkle with cheese and dot
with butter. Bake in a 350° oven
10 to 15 minutes until nicely
browned.

Tortillas Acapulco style

Enchiladas Acapulco

4 servings

 1½ cups hot red sauce
     (recipe page 34)
 12 tortillas (recipe page 37)
  1 cup refried beans
     (recipe page 72)
  1 cup cooked diced veal or
     chicken
  1 cup sour cream

Heat the hot red sauce and
spread each tortilla with a little
of the sauce. Combine the
remaining sauce with the beans
and veal. Reserve ⅓ of the
mixture. Spread each tortilla
with a portion of the
remaining mixture. Roll up the
tortillas and place in a buttered
shallow baking pan. Spread the
remaining mixture over the
tortillas and top with sour
cream. Bake in a 350° oven 15 to
20 minutes. Serve with a crisp
green salad.

Tortillas with eggs farmhouse style

Huevos Rancheros

4 servings

  3 tablespoons oil
  8 tortillas (recipe page 37)
  4 tablespoons butter
  8 eggs
  ⅔ cup hot red sauce
     (recipe page 34)
  1 avocado, thinly sliced

Heat the oil in a skillet and fry
the tortillas, 1 at a time, until
lightly browned on both sides.
Place 2 tortillas on each of 4
serving plates. Melt the butter
and fry the eggs until the whites
are set but the yolks still soft.
Top each tortilla with a fried
egg and garnish with hot red
sauce and avocado slices.
Serve immediately.

*'Huevos rancheros' are, literally,
eggs, farmhouse style – served on
tortillas, garnished with hot
chili sauce and cool avocados.*

Tortillas with eggs farmhouse style

Tacos with chicken

Tacos de gallína

4 to 6 servings

- 4 tablespoons oil
- 2 tablespoons minced onion
- ¼ cup tomato purée
- ¼ cup tomato paste
- 2 cups diced cooked chicken
- 1 canned hot chili pepper, finely chopped
- 2 tablespoons chopped green olives
- ½ teaspoon salt
- 12 tortillas (recipe page 37)
  Lettuce leaves
- 1 avocado, peeled and sliced

Heat 2 tablespoons oil in a saucepan and sauté the onion until golden brown. Add the tomato purée, tomato paste, chicken, chili, olives and salt and stir until the ingredients are heated through. Place a portion of the chicken mixture on each tortilla and roll them up. Heat the remaining oil in a skillet and sauté the tortillas a few minutes until crisp on all sides. Garnish.

Pancakes with cheese

Panquecas com queijo

4 servings

- 2 cups Ricotta cheese
- 2 eggs, lightly beaten
- ¼ cup grated Parmesan cheese
- ½ teaspoon salt
  Freshly ground black pepper
- 2 tablespoons finely chopped parsley
- 1 tablespoon grated onion
- 12 tortillas (recipe page 37)
- 1 cup prepared tomato sauce

Thoroughly combine the Ricotta cheese, eggs, Parmesan cheese, salt, pepper, parsley and onion. Spread a portion of the mixture on each tortilla. Roll up the tortillas and place in a shallow buttered baking dish. Pour the tomato sauce on top. Bake in a 350° oven 10 to 15 minutes until the sauce is bubbling.

Broccoli pancakes

Panquecas de brocoli

6 servings

Filling:
- 1 large bunch broccoli
- 2 tablespoons vinegar
- 4 tablespoons water
- 4 tablespoons butter
- 2 tablespoons finely chopped onion

Meat sauce:
- 2 tablespoons oil
- 1 pound lean ground beef
- 2 tablespoons finely chopped onion
- 1 clove garlic, crushed
- 1 bay leaf, crumbled
- ¼ teaspoon oregano
- 1 tablespoon finely chopped parsley
- 1 tablespoon chopped chives
- 6 tomatoes, peeled, seeded and chopped
- ½ teaspoon salt
  Freshly ground black pepper
- 12 tortillas (recipe page 37)
- 4 tablespoons grated Parmesan cheese

To prepare the filling, divide the broccoli into flowerets. Combine the vinegar and water in a small bowl and dip the flowerets into the mixture several times. Bring plenty of salted water to a boil and cook the broccoli about 7 minutes until barely tender. Drain the broccoli. Heat the butter in a skillet and sauté the onion until soft. Add the broccoli and sauté, stirring with a wooden spoon, 2 or 3 minutes more.

To prepare the meat sauce, heat the oil in a skillet and sauté the beef until it has lost all trace of pink. Pour off all the accumulated fat and add the onion, garlic, bay leaf, oregano, parsley, chives, tomatoes, salt and pepper. Cook over low heat 10 to 15 minutes, stirring occasionally. The sauce will be thick. If it tends to stick to the skillet, add water, 1 tablespoon at a time.

To assemble the dish, roll up the broccoli in the tortillas, leaving a floweret sticking out at each end. Arrange the tortillas in a circle around the edge of an ovenproof serving dish. Mound the meat sauce in the center and sprinkle with cheese. Place in a 350° oven 5 to 10 minutes just until heated through. Serve immediately.

Brazilians excel at subtle spicing. Here, broccoli is cooked and rolled in thin tortillas and garnished with a tomato and herb flavored meat sauce

Broccoli pancakes

Stuffed corn husks 1

Tamales

12 to 16 servings

12 to 16 dried or fresh cornhusks
½ cup lard
2 cups masa harina (corn
  flour)
1 teaspoon salt
½ to ⅔ cup beef broth
1 cup spicy chocolate sauce
  recipe page 36)
½ pound cooked turkey meat,
  diced

Soak the dried cornhusks in
warm water 30 minutes or wash
the fresh corn husks. Beat the
lard with an electric mixer until
light and fluffy. Add the masa
harina and salt and combine
thoroughly. Add enough of the
broth to make a soft dough.
Spread the corn husks out on a
board. They should measure
approximately 4 to 5 inches
wide and 8 inches long. If they
are not wide enough, overlap
2 husks. Spread the dough in a
3 inch square in the center of
each husk. Combine the
sauce and the diced turkey and
place a mound of the mixture
on top of the dough. Fold over
each long, narrow edge, then
fold in thirds, enclosing the
filling. Place the tamales, seam
side down, in a steamer or
colander. Steam over simmering
water 1 hour. Serve immediately.

*All through Latin America there
are variations of the cornhusk,
stuffed with meat, meal,
vegetables, spices – all carefully
wrapped and steamed to delicate
tenderness. These tamales are
typical of Mexico.*

Corn bread pudding

Pan de maiz

8 to 10 servings

3 tablespoons olive oil
3 onions, finely chopped
3 tomatoes, peeled, seeded
  and chopped
¾ cup chicken broth
1 teaspoon salt
2 cups sifted corn meal
1 teaspoon baking powder
½ pound cottage cheese
3 tablespoons melted butter
1½ cups milk

Heat the olive oil in a saucepan
and sauté the onions 5 minutes.
Add the tomatoes and cook
10 minutes, stirring frequently.
Add the broth and salt and
cook over medium heat 10
minutes. Sift the corn meal
and baking powder together
into a bowl. Add the cottage
cheese, butter and milk and
mix thoroughly. Stir in the
onion/tomato mixture. Place in
a buttered 8 × 8 inch baking
pan and bake the pudding in a
350° oven 1 hour. Cut into
rectangles and serve immediately.

Corn bread

Chepa

⅔ cup butter
2 eggs
1½ cups grated sharp Cheddar
  cheese
2¼ cups yellow corn meal
½ teaspoon salt
2 teaspoons baking powder
⅓ cup milk

Beat the butter until light and
fluffy. Add the eggs 1 at a time,
beating well after each addition.
Add the cheese and beat until
the mixture is smooth. Combine
the corn meal, salt and baking
powder and add to the cheese
mixture alternately with the
milk. Continue beating until
well blended. Spread the batter
in a buttered 8 inch loaf pan and
cover with aluminum foil. Bake
in a 375° oven 50 to 60 minutes
or until the loaf is firm. Remove
from the pan and cool on a wire
rack.

Stuffed corn husks 2

Humitas

4 to 6 servings

4 to 6 fresh corn husks
4 cups (8 ears) fresh corn
  kernels
3 tablespoons butter
1 onion, chopped
1 tomato, peeled, seeded
  and chopped
½ teaspoon salt
  Freshly ground black pepper
1 teaspoon sugar
¼ cup milk
2 eggs

Remove the corn kernels from
the cobs. Reserve the cobs.
Keep the largest husks (leaves
from the corn cobs) and cover
with boiling water to soften.
Heat the butter in a frying pan,
add the onion and fry for
5 minutes until soft. Add the
tomato, salt, pepper and sugar
and cook for 5 minutes. Add
the corn, milk and eggs and
cook gently for 10 minutes,
stirring constantly. Dry the
corn husks and place 3
tablespoons of the mixture in
the center of each. If husks
are small, use 2 for each
humitas. Fold the sides of the
husks over the filling and lap
the two ends over each other
to enclose the filling. Secure
tightly with string. Arrange
the cobs on the bottom of a
large wide pan and barely
cover with boiling water.
Cover with the humitas.
Cover the pan tightly so that
steam cannot escape and cook
30 minutes. Remove from the
heat, untie and stack on hot
platter without opening the husks.

Stuffed corn husks

Rice Mexican style

Arroz a la mexicana

4 servings

  3 *tablespoons oil*
  1 *large onion, chopped*
1½ *cups rice*
  3 *cups chicken broth*
  4 *large tomatoes, peeled,*
     seeded and chopped
  2 *red chilies, mashed*
  1 *clove garlic, crushed*
 ½ *teaspoon salt*

Heat the oil in a saucepan, add the onion and fry for 5 minutes until golden brown. Add the rice and stir for 2 minutes. Add the chicken broth, tomatoes, chilies, garlic and salt. Cover and simmer gently for 25 minutes until the rice is tender and has absorbed the liquid. Serve with a salad or tomatoes.

Rice with sour cream

Arroz jocqui

4 servings

  2 *cups cooked rice*
 ½ *cup diced cooked chicken*
 ½ *cup diced cooked ham*
 ½ *teaspoon salt*
     Freshly ground black pepper
  2 *cups sour cream*
  2 *sweet green peppers,*
     seeded and cut into pieces
  3 *tablespoons tomato catsup*
 ½ *pound Ricotta cheese*
  6 *tablespoons grated Parmesan*
     cheese

Combine the rice with the chicken and ham. Season with salt and pepper. Mix the sour cream with the green peppers and tomato catsup. Alternate layers of rice, sour cream mixture and Ricotta cheese in a buttered fireproof dish. Top with a layer of rice. Sprinkle with Parmesan cheese. Bake in a preheated 350° oven for 30 minutes until the cheese has melted and browned.

Green rice

Arroz verde

4 servings

  2 *green peppers, seeded and*
     finely chopped
  1 *chili poblano, peeled, seeded*
     and finely chopped
  1 *cup chopped parsley*
  1 *green onion, chopped*
  1 *clove garlic*
  3 *cups chicken broth*
  3 *tablespoons oil*
1½ *cups raw rice*
  3 *hard boiled eggs, sliced*
  2 *small cans sardines, drained*

Combine the green peppers, chili poblano, ½ cup parsley, onion and garlic in an electric blender. Blend to form a smooth purée. Add the chicken broth and mix well. Heat the oil in a saucepan. Add the rice, stirring constantly until the rice is lightly browned. Add the purée, cover, and cook gently for 20 minutes until the rice is tender. Transfer to a warm serving dish and sprinkle with the remaining parsley. Garnish with sliced eggs and sardines and serve hot.

Molded rice

Angú

4 to 6 servings

  2 *cups water*
  1 *cup coconut milk (see note)*
1½ *cups rice flour*
 ½ *teaspoon salt*

Combine water and coconut milk. Place 2 cups of the mixture in a saucepan and bring to a simmer. Combine the rice flour with the remaining liquid and beat with a wire whisk until smooth. Add the flour paste to the simmering liquid, a little at a time, stirring constantly with a wire whisk. Boil 5 minutes, stirring constantly. Lower the heat and simmer 15 minutes, stirring occasionally. Season with salt. This dish is traditionally placed in a mold, chilled and served cold, but most Americans prefer it served hot like a thick cereal.
Note: To make coconut milk, simmer together equal parts of shredded dried coconut and milk for 30 minutes. Strain and use the milk as directed.

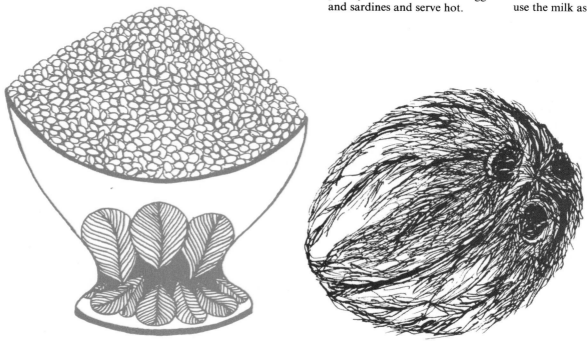

Mexican corn pie

Tamale pastel

4 servings

  2 *tablespoons olive oil*
  2 *onions, chopped*
  1 *clove garlic, crushed*
  2 *cups diced cooked pork*
  1 *teaspoon chili powder*
  ⅓ *cup chopped pitted olives*
  ¼ *teaspoon coriander*
  ½ *teaspoon salt*
  4 *small tomatoes, peeled,*
    seeded and chopped
  1 *cup beef broth*
  ½ *cup water*
  ¾ *cup masa harina (corn flour)*
  6 *slices Muenster cheese*

Heat the oil in a heavy frying pan, add the onions and garlic and cook for 5 minutes until soft and golden. Add the diced pork, chili powder, olives, coriander, salt, tomatoes and beef broth. Simmer for 10 minutes. Combine the water and masa harina and add to the pan. Bring to a boil, stirring constantly, and cook for 5 minutes. Turn into a buttered 8 inch square baking dish and cover with slices of cheese. Bake in a preheated 350° oven for 30 minutes and serve hot.

Chilean corn pie

Pastel de choclo

6 servings

  4 *tablespoons oil*
  1 *onion, chopped*
  ½ *pound ground beef*
  ¼ *teaspoon thyme*
  ½ *teaspoon salt*
    Freshly ground black pepper
  3 *hard boiled eggs, sliced*
  ¼ *cup raisins*
  2 *cups diced cooked chicken*
  1½ *cups frozen or canned corn*
  1 *cup milk*
  2 *eggs, beaten*
  ½ *teaspoon basil*
  1 *teaspoon sugar*
  2 *tablespoons butter*

Heat the oil in a frying pan, add the onion and fry for 5 minutes until soft and golden. Add the ground beef, thyme, salt and pepper and cook for 10 minutes, stirring occasionally. Place in a buttered ovenproof casserole. Arrange a layer of egg slices over the meat, sprinkle with raisins and cover with the chicken. Cook the corn in the milk for 5 minutes. Cool. Add the beaten eggs, basil and sugar. Pour over the chicken, dot with butter and bake in a preheated 350° oven for 30 minutes.

Pasta is popular in Paraguay – thanks to the Italian immigrants there. Here it is served with mushrooms and spicy sausage.

Noodles with mushroom sauce

Noodles with mushroom sauce

Tallarines con salsa de hongos

4 servings

  3 *slices bacon, chopped*
  2 *onions, finely chopped*
  1 *cup tomato sauce*
  1 *tomato, peeled, seeded*
    and chopped
  ¼ *pound ham, cut into*
    thin strips
  2 *Spanish sausages or*
    substitute pepperoni
  ½ *teaspoon salt*
    Freshly ground black pepper
  1 *cup mushrooms*
  1 *cup beef broth*
  ¾ *pound noodles, cooked*
    until barely tender and
    drained
  1 *cup grated Parmesan cheese*

Fry the bacon in a saucepan until the fat has rendered. Add the onions and fry until golden brown. Add the tomato sauce, tomato, ham, sausages, salt and pepper and combine thoroughly. Cover and simmer 20 minutes. Add the mushrooms and broth and simmer, uncovered, 15 minutes more. Make a layer of noodles in a shallow buttered baking dish. Sprinkle with some of the cheese and spread with part of the sauce. Continue layering until all the ingredients are used, ending with a layer of sauce. Bake in a 375° oven 25 minutes. Serve from the baking dish.

Rice with ham and pineapple

Yambalaya

4 to 6 servings

       6 tablespoons oil
       1 pound cooked ham, cubed
       1 onion, chopped
       2 cloves garlic, crushed
       1 tomato, peeled, seeded and
          sliced
       1 bouillon cube
       1 teaspoon saffron (optional)
       2 cups rice
       3 cups water
       1 teaspoon salt
          Freshly ground black pepper
       1 cup canned shrimp (drain
          and reserve juice)
       1 (1 pound) can sliced
          pineapple (drain and reserve
          juice)
       1 egg, lightly beaten
     ½ cup fine dry breadcrumbs
       4 tablespoons butter

Heat the oil in a saucepan and
and fry the ham for 5 minutes.
Add the onion and garlic and
fry 5 minutes until soft and
golden. Add tomato and
bouillon cube and simmer for 5
minutes more. Add saffron,
rice, water, salt, pepper and the
juices from the pineapple and
shrimp. Cook over low heat for
25 minutes or until the rice is
tender. Stir in the shrimp and
mix well. Dry the slices of
pineapple, dip in beaten egg
and breadcrumbs. Heat the
butter in a frying pan and fry the
pineapple slices until golden
brown. Transfer the rice to a
heated serving dish, garnish
with pineapple slices and serve
hot.

*Rice, subtly spiked with glowing
pink ham is topped with crisply
sautéed pineapple rings in this
uniquely Jamaican way of cooking.*

Fish dishes

In Mexico, delicate lightly sautéed fish fillets are marinated in an orange juice/oil mixture and garnished with green pepper and fragrant orange rind

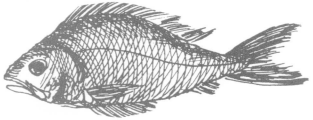

Pickled fish—see recipe page 45

Latin America encompasses more than seven thousand miles of coastline with two oceans, the Gulf of Mexico and the Caribbean Sea to provide a seemingly endless variety of gifts from the sea. Quite naturally, fish is the major protein in most of the coastal countries. Few things equal the glory of fresh-caught fish, quickly cooked – either simply broiled over an open fire on a beach; or stewed with fresh vegetables and spices for a family meal. The cooks of Latin America have developed an infinite number of ways to prepare their natural glory. Pickled, smoked, curried, stewed, stuffed, sauced (often with other fish), fish in the countries of Latin America reaches a peak of perfection seldom found in any other part of the world.
Of particular note is the great supply of red snapper available throughout Mexico – often served with sweet and sour sauce that defies analysis. All through the Caribbean areas, the fish markets are one of the great 'tourista' sights. The great variety of seafood is attractively arranged and garnished and the vendors sing the special charms of their particular catch each morning. The Amazon and the River Plata also supply a great abundance of fish. Shellfish – the huge shrimp, and lobsters caught off the coast of Chile and Peru – are famous all over the world.
The breading and frying techniques so common in North America are seldom found in the southern countries where the cooks understand the need to maintain the delicate, natural flavor of fish or to enchance it only lightly.

Pickled fish

Escabeche de pescado

4 servings

- 3 tablespoons butter
- 2 pounds fish fillets
- ¼ cup olive oil
- ¼ cup orange juice
- 3 tablespoons tarragon vinegar
- 2 bay leaves
- 1 teaspoon salt
- ⅛ teaspoon white pepper
  Rind of 2 oranges
- 1 green pepper, seeded and cut in strips
- 2 tablespoons finely chopped scallion
- 1 small clove garlic, crushed
- 1 teaspoon tarragon

Heat the butter in a skillet and brown the fish fillets quickly on both sides. Carefully transfer the fish to a shallow glass dish. Combine the remaining ingredients and pour over the fish. Cover tightly with plastic wrap and refrigerate at least 12 hours, basting occasionally

Fish balls

Curried fish

Massala viesie

4 servings

- 4 fillets of cod, halibut or snapper
- 1 teaspoon salt
- 6 tablespoons oil
- 1 onion, chopped
- 2 cloves garlic, crushed
- 1 tomato, peeled, seeded and chopped
- 1 green pepper, seeded and cut into pieces
- 1 to 3 teaspoons curry powder, to taste
- 1 cup water

Dry the fish with paper towels and season with salt. Heat the oil in a frying pan and brown the fish 5 minutes on each side. Remove the fish from the pan. Add the onion and garlic to the same oil and fry for 5 minutes. Add the tomato, pepper and curry and cook for 5 minutes more. Return the fish to the pan. Add the water and simmer, covered, for 15 minutes. Serve the fish with rice.

Fish balls

Balchi di pisca

4 servings

- 2 cups water
- ¾ teaspoon salt
- 1 pound fish fillets
- 2 slices day old, firm textured white bread, crusts removed
- ½ cup milk
- 1 egg, lightly beaten
- 1½ tablespoons tomato purée
  Freshly ground black pepper
- 1 cup fine dry breadcrumbs
- 4 tablespoons oil

Bring the water to a simmer and add ½ teaspoon salt and the fish fillets. Cook gently 8 minutes or until the fish is tender. Remove the fish with a slotted spoon and pat dry with paper towels. Flake the fish finely with a fork and place in a bowl. Soak the bread in the milk 5 minutes. Squeeze out the excess milk and crumble the bread into the bowl. Add the egg, tomato purée, remaining salt and pepper and combine thoroughly. Shape the mixture into walnut sized balls and coat with breadcrumbs. Heat the oil in a skillet and sauté the fish balls until golden brown on all sides. Remove them with a slotted spoon and drain on paper towels. Serve immediately.

Fish is sometimes finely chopped with seasoning, then fried quickly to preserve its delicacy.

Pickled raw fish

Peruvian pickled fish

Cebiche

6 servings

   6 *fillets of sole, cut into*
     thin strips
   1 *cup dry white wine*
   1 *cup lemon juice*
   3 *onions, thinly sliced*
   2 *teaspoons salt*
   1 *cup water*
  ½ *cup vinegar*
   2 *chili peppers minced or*
  ½ *teaspoon chili powder*
  ¼ *teaspoon freshly ground*
     black pepper
   3 *cooked sweet potatoes, sliced*
     Lettuce leaves

Place the fish in a bowl and add
the wine and lemon juice. Let
stand 3 hours at room
temperature. Place the onions
in a separate bowl. Add
1 teaspoon salt and the water
and soak 20 minutes. Drain
and rinse the onions under
cold running water. Return
the onions to the bowl. Add the
vinegar and soak 1 hour.
Drain and toss with the chili
peppers, black pepper and
remaining salt. Gently combine
the onion mixture with the fish
and let marinate 2 hours more.
Refrigerate 2 to 3 hours before
serving. Serve garnished with
sliced sweet potatoes and
lettuce leaves.

Cebiche de corvina

6 servings

   2 *pounds hake or other white*
     fish fillets
   1 *teaspoon salt*
     Freshly ground black pepper
   2 *whole hot chili peppers,*
     seeded and sliced into thin
     strips
   1 *tablespoon chili powder*
   2 *large onions, finely chopped*
     Juice of 3 lemons
     Juice of 4 limes
   1 *head of lettuce*
   1 *pound sweet potatoes, cooked*
     and sliced
   4 *ears fresh corn, cooked and*
     cut into 2 inch rounds

Cut the fish into 1 inch pieces
and place in a large flat glass or
ceramic dish. Mix the salt,
pepper and the chili peppers.
Add the chili powder and
onions and combine with the
fish. Add the lemon and lime
juices and stir carefully so that
fish does not break. If the
marinade does not cover the
fish, add additional lemon or
lime juice. Cover and
refrigerate 3 to 4 hours or
overnight. When ready to serve,
place the raw fish on a bed of
lettuce leaves. Serve with the
hot slices of sweet potato and
rings of corn on the cob.

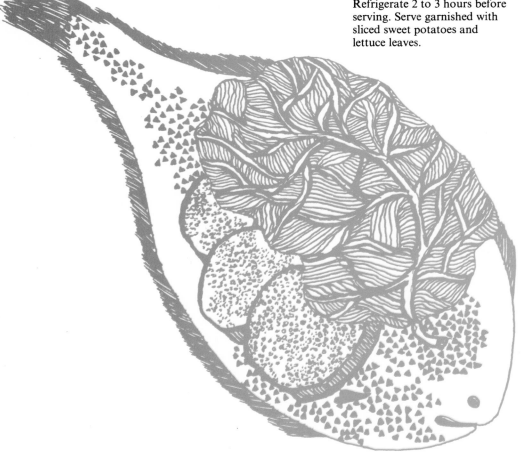

Pickled mackerel

Fish stew

Fish casserole

Pejerrey en escabeche

4 servings

2 pounds mackerel fillets
1 cup oil
½ cup vinegar
2 onions, sliced
1 clove garlic, crushed
5 cooked carrots, sliced
1 green pepper, seeded and
  cut into strips
1 lemon, sliced
¼ teaspoon thyme
¼ teaspoon sage
½ teaspoon dry mustard
½ teaspoon salt
  Freshly ground black pepper

Sauté the mackerel fillets in
3 tablespoons of oil for about
15 seconds on each side.
Transfer to a shallow pan.
Place the remaining ingredients
in a saucepan. Bring to a boil
and pour over the fish. Cover
with plastic wrap and
refrigerate several days
before serving.

Vatapa

8 servings

3 cups unsweetened grated
  coconut
3 cups milk
4 tablespoons olive oil
2 onions, finely chopped
2 cloves garlic, crushed
½ teaspoon chili powder
4 tomatoes, chopped
2 cups water
2 teaspoons salt
1 teaspoon ginger
2 bay leaves
2 pounds fish fillets (cod or
  halibut), 4 inch pieces
1 pound shrimp, shelled and
  deveined
1 cup ground unsalted peanuts
6 tablespoons corn meal

Place the coconut and milk in a
saucepan and simmer over the
lowest possible heat 30 minutes.
Strain and reserve the milk.
Heat the oil in a large saucepan
and sauté the onions and garlic

until golden brown. Add the
chili powder and tomatoes and
simmer 5 minutes. Add the
water, salt, ginger and bay
leaves and bring to a boil.
Lower the heat, add the fish
fillets and shrimp and simmer
3 to 5 minutes. Transfer the fish
and shrimp to a plate. Strain
and reserve the broth. Place the
reserved milk in a large
saucepan, add the peanuts and
simmer 15 minutes. Add the
reserved fish broth and stir in
corn meal. Simmer 25 minutes,
stirring frequently. Add fish and
shrimp and simmer until heated
through. Serve over rice.

Pisca stoba

4 servings

2 tablespoons butter
1 onion, thinly sliced and
  separated into rings
2 cloves garlic, crushed
1 green pepper, seeded and
  chopped
1 tomato, peeled, seeded and
  chopped
1 teaspoon salt
  Large pinch of saffron
1 cup water
4 small cooked potatoes,
  cubed
4 fish fillets (halibut, cod,
  red snapper

Heat the butter in a casserole.
Add the onion, garlic, green
pepper and tomato and cook,
stirring, 2 minutes. Add the
salt, saffron and water and
bring to a boil. Lower the heat,
cover and simmer 30 minutes.
Add the potatoes and fish and
simmer 10 to 15 minutes,
depending on the thickness of
the fish fillets. Do not overcook
the fish. Serve from
the casserole.

Fish casserole

*Island cooks combine native fish,
vegetables and saffron in the
Antilles.*

Baked fish fillets

Pescado al horno

6 servings

  6 tablespoons butter
  2 onions, chopped
2½ cups fresh breadcrumbs
  3 egg yolks, beaten
  2 tablespoons heavy cream
½ cup sherry
1½ teaspoons salt
    Freshly ground black pepper
¼ teaspoon nutmeg
  6 fillets of sole or flounder

Heat 4 tablespoons butter in a frying pan. Add the onions and fry for 10 minutes until soft and golden. Add the breadcrumbs, egg yolks, cream, ¼ cup sherry, 1 teaspoon salt, pepper and nutmeg. Stir until well blended. Divide the mixture evenly over the 6 fish fillets and roll each one up. Secure with a toothpick. Melt the remaining butter in a baking dish and arrange the fish in the bottom. Sprinkle with the remaining salt, pepper and sherry. Bake in a preheated 400° oven for 25 minutes, basting with the sauce. Serve with boiled potatoes and a dry white wine.

Delicate fillets of local fish are wrapped around a creamy egg yolk filling and baked in a simple sauce for a delectable dish in Bolivia.

Fish fillets in wine sauce

Filet de peixe à Marguery

4 servings

  2 pounds fillet of sole
  1 teaspoon salt
    Freshly ground black pepper
1½ cups dry white wine
  1 cup sliced mushrooms
  2 tablespoons butter
  3 tablespoons flour
  1 egg yolk
½ cup heavy cream
    Juice of ½ lemon
  1 cup cooked small shrimp

Sprinkle the fillets of sole with ½ teaspoon salt and pepper. Fold them in half and place in a buttered heatproof casserole. Add ½ cup wine. Bring to a simmer, cover and cook 8 minutes until the fish is just done. Do not overcook. Drain the fillets and arrange in an ovenproof serving dish. Cook the mushrooms in boiling salted water 2 minutes. Drain and place on top of the fish. Melt the butter in a saucepan. Add the flour and cook, stirring, 1 minute. Add the remaining wine gradually, stirring constantly, until the sauce is thickened and smooth. Beat the egg yolk with the cream in a mixing bowl. Add the hot sauce a little at a time, beating constantly with a wire whisk. When ¾ of the hot sauce has been added, pour the mixture back into the saucepan. Bring to a simmer and stir in the lemon juice and remaining salt and pepper. Sprinkle the shrimp over the fish and pour the sauce over all. Place in a 350° oven 5 to 10 minutes until heated through. Serve immediately.

Baked fish fillets

Baked whiting

Pescadilla al horno

4 servings

- 1 (3 pound) whiting
- 2 cups freshly made breadcrumbs
- 1 cup milk
- 1 onion, grated
- 2 tablespoons finely chopped parsley
- 1 egg yolk
- ½ teaspoon salt
  Freshly ground black pepper
- 1 onion, sliced
- 1 stalk celery, sliced
- 6 parsley stems
- 4 slices lemon
- ¼ cup olive oil
  Juice of 2 lemons
- ½ cup dry white wine

Have the fishman clean the fish but leave the head and tail intact. Soak the breadcrumbs in the milk 10 minutes. Squeeze out the excess milk and place the breadcrumbs in a bowl. Add the grated onion, parsley, egg yolk, salt and pepper and combine thoroughly. Stuff the fish with the mixture and secure the opening with skewers or thread. Pass a trussing needle threaded with string through the head and tail of the fish and gently pull it into a semicircle. Knot the string to hold the fish in that position. Scatter the sliced onion, celery, parsley and lemon slices on the bottom of a baking dish. Place the fish on top of the vegetables and pour over the olive oil, lemon juice and wine. Bake in a 400° oven about 25 to 30 minutes until the fish flakes easily with a fork. Baste frequently with the pan juices. Place the fish on a heated platter and remove the string and trussing skewers. Strain the cooking liquid over the fish and serve immediately.

Cod Argentine style

Bacalao a la argentina

6 servings

- 1½ pounds dried salt cod
- 1 onion
- 1 bay leaf
- ½ cup olive oil
- 3 onions, chopped
- 1 clove garlic, crushed
- 2 cups cooked chick peas
- 3 eggs
- 3 tablespoons lemon juice
- ¼ teaspoon chili powder
- 4 tablespoons grated Parmesan cheese
- 4 tablespoons finely chopped parsley
- ½ cup fine dry breadcrumbs
- 2 tablespoons butter
- 12 olives, pitted

Soak the cod for 12 hours in cold water. Change the water twice. Drain. Cover the fish with fresh water and add the onion and bay leaf. Bring to a boil, reduce the heat and simmer for 30 minutes. Drain and flake the fish finely with a fork. Heat 4 tablespoons oil in a saucepan, add the chopped onions and garlic and fry for 5 minutes until golden. Add the flaked cod and chick peas and mix well. Spread in a buttered ovenproof dish. Beat the eggs and add the remaining olive oil gradually. Stir in the lemon juice, chili powder, grated cheese and parsley. Pour this mixture over the fish, cover with breadcrumbs and dot with butter. Bake in a preheated 350° oven for 20 minutes. Garnish with olives and serve from the dish.

Stuffed fish

Huachinango relleno

6 servings

- 6 tablespoons butter
- 3 tablespoons flour
- ¾ cup chicken broth
- ¾ cup light cream
- ¼ teaspoon salt
  Freshly ground black pepper
  Juice of ½ lemon
- 1 cup sliced mushrooms
- 12 cooked mussels, sliced
- 6 fillets of sole
- 2 tablespoons finely chopped parsley

Heat 3 tablespoons butter in a saucepan. Add the flour and cook, stirring, 1 minute. Add the broth and cream gradually, stirring constantly until the sauce is thick and smooth. Season with salt, pepper and lemon juice. Heat the remaining butter in a skillet and sauté the mushrooms 2 or 3 minutes over high heat. Remove from the heat and combine the mushrooms with the mussels and ½ cup of the sauce. Sprinkle the fillets with salt and pepper and spread each with a portion of the stuffing. Roll up the fillets and tie with string. Place in a buttered shallow baking dish and top with the remaining sauce. Bake in a 375° oven 15 to 20 minutes. Garnish with chopped parsley and serve with rice.

Fish Veracruz style

Huachinango a la veracruzana

4 servings

- 1 (2 pound) red snapper or other fish
- 1 teaspoon salt
- 1 clove garlic, crushed
- 4 tablespoons olive oil
- 1 onion, chopped
- 5 tomatoes, peeled, seeded and chopped
- ¼ teaspoon cinnamon
- ¼ teaspoon cloves
- ⅓ cup jalapeno pepper (canned hot chili), seeded and cut into strips
- 3 tablespoons capers
- 1 tablespoon lemon juice
- ⅓ cup stuffed olives, halved

Clean the fish and rub with salt and garlic. Heat the oil, add the onion and fry 5 minutes until soft and golden. Add the tomatoes, cinnamon and cloves and simmer gently for 5 minutes. Place the fish in a buttered ovenproof dish and cover with the jalapeno pepper, capers, lemon juice and olives. Cover with the tomato mixture. Bake in a preheated 350° oven for 30 to 40 minutes until the fish is tender. Serve with refried beans and crisp tortillas.

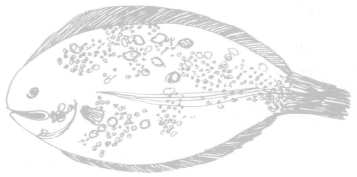

Fish prepared with fruit juice

Pescado en jugo de fruta

3 servings

- 2 *tablespoons oil*
- 1 *large onion, chopped*
- ½ *cup black olives, pitted and cut into quarters*
- ½ *cup red pepper, chopped*
- 1 *teaspoon dried coriander*
- ½ *teaspoon salt*
  Freshly ground black pepper
- 4 *tablespoons orange juice*
- 2 *tablespoons lemon juice*
- 1 *tablespoon butter*
- 3 *(¾ pound) whole fish*
  Whites of 3 hard boiled eggs, chopped

Heat the oil, add the onion and fry for 5 minutes until soft. Add the olives, red pepper, coriander, salt, pepper and fruit juices. Melt the butter in an ovenproof casserole, add the fish and pour the sauce over. Bake in a preheated 350° oven for 15 minutes or until the fish is tender. Baste with the sauce occasionally during cooking. Garnish with the chopped egg whites and serve hot.

Corbina baked with egg

Corvina al horno con salsa de huevo

4 servings

- 4 *(½ pound) pieces corbina or halibut*
- ½ *teaspoon salt*
  Freshly ground black pepper
  Juice of 1 lemon
- 1 *onion, sliced*
- ½ *cup olive oil*
- 2 *egg yolks*

Sprinkle the fish on both sides with salt, pepper and lemon juice and place in a shallow ovenproof casserole. Arrange the onion slices on top of the fish and pour on the olive oil. Bake in a 350° oven about 12 minutes or until the fish flakes easily with a fork. Transfer the fish to a heated serving plate and strain the pan liquid into a small saucepan. Beat the egg yolks into the liquid and place over very low heat, beating constantly with a wire whisk just until the mixture thickens. Immediately remove from the heat. Spoon the sauce over fish

Molded salt cod with shrimp sauce

Pudim de bacalhau

6 servings

- ¾ *pound salt cod*
- 3 *tablespoons oil*
- 1 *onion, finely chopped*
- 2 *tomatoes, peeled, seeded and chopped*
- ¼ *cup dry white wine*
- 4 *tablespoons butter*
- 6 *tablespoons flour*
- 1¾ *cups milk*
- 4 *eggs, separated*
- ½ *cup raisins*
  Freshly ground black pepper
- 2 *tablespoons finely chopped parsley*
- 2 *small onions, thinly sliced*
- 5 *pimiento stuffed olives, thinly sliced*

Soak the cod in cold water overnight, changing the water several times. Remove any skin and bones and grind the cod in a blender or use the finest blade of a meat grinder. Heat the oil in a skillet and sauté the onion, tomatoes and cod for 5 minutes over medium heat. Add the wine and simmer 5 minutes. Meanwhile, heat the butter in a saucepan. Add the flour and cook, stirring, 2 minutes. Add the milk gradually, stirring constantly until the mixture is very thick. Remove from the heat and beat in the egg yolks, 1 at a time. Stir in the raisins, pepper, parsley and cod mixture. Beat the egg whites until soft peaks form. Stir ⅓ of the whites into the cod mixture and carefully fold in the remainder. Butter and flour a 2 quart ovenproof mold. Transfer the cod mixture to the mold and place it in a larger pan of hot water to come ⅔ of the way up the sides of the mold. Bake in a 350° oven 1½ hours or until a knife inserted in the center comes out clean. Remove from the oven and let stand 10 minutes. Unmold the cod onto a serving plate and decorate with thinly sliced onions and olives. Serve with a shrimp sauce (page 35).

Fish prepared with fruit juice

Shrimp pie

Empadinhas de camarão

4 to 6 servings

Pastry:
2½ cups flour
½ teaspoon salt
6 tablespoons butter, cut into small pieces
6 tablespoons shortening
2 egg yolks
4 to 5 tablespoons ice water

Filling:
2 tablespoons oil
1 onion, chopped
1 clove garlic, crushed
4 medium sized tomatoes, peeled and chopped
1½ cups (1 pound) shrimp, cooked and chopped
1 teaspoon salt
Freshly ground black pepper
¼ cup chopped ripe olives
1 hard boiled egg, chopped
2 tablespoons chopped parsley
1 egg yolk, lightly beaten

To prepare the pastry, measure the flour and salt into a bowl. Add the butter and shortening. Combine with a pastry blender or fingertips. Add the egg yolks. Add the water, a little at a time, and stir with a fork to form the pastry into a ball. Wrap in waxed paper and chill for 20 minutes. Cut the dough in half. Roll each half on a lightly floured board to fit a 9 inch pie plate. To prepare the filling, heat the oil in a saucepan, add the onion and garlic and cook over low heat for 10 minutes until the onion is soft and golden. Add the tomatoes and cook for 10 minutes. Add the shrimp, salt, pepper, olives, chopped egg and parsley. Let the filling cool for 15 minutes. Pour into the pastry shell and cover with the remaining circle of pastry. Brush with beaten egg yolk. Bake in a preheated 400° oven for 35 minutes or until golden brown on top. Serve hot.

Fried fish in escabeche sauce

Peixe escabeche a moda Brasileira

4 servings

1 tomato, peeled, seeded and chopped
1 onion, cut into thin slices
1 tablespoon chopped coriander or
1 teaspoon dried coriander
1 tablespoon chopped parsley
1 tablespoon chopped chives
2 tablespoons oil
1 tablespoon vinegar
1 clove garlic, crushed
1 cup water
½ teaspoon salt
Freshly ground black pepper
¼ cup oil
1½ pounds fillets of white fish

Prepare the sauce by mixing all the ingredients together, except for the oil and fish. Bring to a boil and simmer for 10 minutes. Keep warm. Heat the ¼ cup oil in a frying pan, add the fish and fry over high heat for 5 minutes on each side. Add the sauce and simmer for 5 minutes. May be accompanied by fluffy rice.

Shrimp in curry sauce

Shrimp in curry sauce

Sara Sara

4 servings

6 tablespoons oil
12 jumbo shrimp, shelled and deveined
4 cloves garlic, crushed
1 fresh red pepper, seeded and cut into small pieces
1 onion, chopped
⅓ teaspoon salt
1 to 3 teaspoons curry powder, to taste
1 tomato, peeled, seeded and sliced
2 tablespoons chopped parsley or celery leaves

Heat the oil in a frying pan and fry the shrimp on both sides for 5 minutes. Reduce the heat, and add the garlic, red pepper, onion, salt, curry and tomato. Simmer for 10 minutes. Sprinkle with chopped parsley or celery leaves before serving.

Shrimp in almond sauce

Camarones con salsa de almendras

4 to 6 servings

2 pounds shrimp
4 cups water
1 stalk celery, sliced
1 teaspoon pickling spices
2 teaspoons salt
5 slices firm textured white bread, crusts removed
1½ cups milk
4 tablespoons butter
2 medium sized onions, finely chopped
2 cloves garlic, crushed
1 teaspoon paprika
¼ teaspoon chili powder
Freshly ground black pepper
1 cup finely ground almonds

Wash the shrimp. Place the water, celery, pickling spices and 1 teaspoon salt in a large saucepan and bring to a boil. Add the shrimp, cover and cook 3 to 4 minutes. Drain the shrimp in a colander and reserve 1½ cups of the liquid. Shell and devein the shrimp and dry thoroughly on paper towels. Soak the bread in the milk 5 minutes. Remove, reserving milk, and mash the bread until fairly smooth. Heat the butter in a large skillet. Add the onions, garlic, paprika, chili powder, remaining salt and pepper and cook over medium heat about 10 minutes until the onions are very soft. Add the bread and cook, stirring, 5 minutes. Add the almonds, milk in which the bread has been soaked and the reserved shrimp cooking liquid and stir until thickened. Add the shrimp and continue stirring 5 minutes or until the shrimp are heated through. Serve immediately.

The beautiful big shrimp of the Caribbean are sweet and rich. In the Guyanas they are fried quickly, then simmered briefly in a pungent curry sauce.

Shrimp Bahia style in tomato sauce

Camarão à Bahiana

4 servings

>   3 tablespoons oil
>   1 onion, finely chopped
>   6 small tomatoes, peeled,
>   seeded and chopped
>   ¼ cup finely chopped parsley
>   2 pounds shrimp, shelled and
>   deveined
>   ½ teaspoon salt
>   Freshly ground black pepper
>   1 tablespoon butter
>   1 tablespoon flour
>   1 cup coconut milk (see note)
>   2 small very hot red peppers,
>   minced (optional)

Heat the oil in a large saucepan and sauté the onion until softened. Add the tomatoes and parsley and sauté 5 minutes. Add the shrimp and cook, stirring constantly, 3 minutes. Season with salt and pepper. In a small saucepan, melt the butter. Add the flour and cook, stirring, 1 minute. Add the coconut milk gradually, stirring constantly until slightly thickened. Add the sauce and peppers to the shrimp mixture. Simmer 2 minutes. Transfer to a heated serving dish and surround with fried rice.
Note: To make coconut milk, simmer equal amounts of grated unsweetened coconut and milk together for 30 minutes. Strain the milk and use as directed.

Brazil's African influence is evident in this peppery shrimp and rice dish.

Shrimp and scallop stew

Chupe de mariscos

4 to 6 servings

- 1 cup water
- 1 cup dry white wine
- 1 pound shrimp, shelled and deveined
- 1 pound scallops
- 1½ cups freshly made breadcrumbs
- 1 cup milk
- 4 tablespoons butter
- 3 onions, finely chopped
- 1 teaspoon paprika
- 1 cup heavy cream
- ¼ teaspoon chili powder
- ½ teaspoon salt
  Freshly ground black pepper
- 3 hard boiled eggs, quartered
- ½ cup grated Parmesan cheese

Bring the water and wine to a boil in a saucepan. Add the shrimp and scallops. Cover and simmer 3 minutes. Drain the shellfish and reserve 1 cup of the liquid. Chop all but 4 of the shrimp and scallops. Soak the breadcrumbs in the milk 10 minutes. Squeeze out the excess milk and discard. Heat the butter in a large skillet. Add the onions and paprika and sauté over moderate heat 10 minutes, stirring frequently. Add the breadcrumbs and reserved shellfish cooking liquid and combine thoroughly. Stir in the chopped shellfish, cream, chili powder, salt and pepper. Cook over the lowest possible heat 10 minutes, stirring frequently. Garnish with hard boiled eggs and Parmesan cheese. Cut reserved shrimp and scallops in half and arrange on top of each serving.

Conger eel in casserole

Congrio a la cacerola

4 servings

- 2 pounds conger eel
- 1 teaspoon salt
  Freshly ground black pepper
- 2 tablespoons oil
- 2 tablespoons lard
- 2 tablespoons butter
- 2 onions, chopped
- 2 cloves garlic, crushed
- ½ teaspoon marjoram
- ½ teaspoon cumin
- 4 medium sized tomatoes, peeled, seeded and thinly sliced
- 4 medium sized potatoes, peeled and thickly sliced
- ¾ cup corn, canned or frozen
- ¼ cup cream
- ¼ cup croutons
- 2 tablespoons chopped parsley

Cut the eel into serving pieces. Season with salt and pepper and brown lightly in the heated oil. Heat the lard and butter in a saucepan. Add the onions, garlic, marjoram and cumin. Fry gently until the onions have softened. Add the tomatoes, potatoes, corn and cream. Cover and cook 20 minutes over low heat. Place ½ of the vegetables and sauce in a casserole. Cover with the eel and top with the remaining vegetables and sauce. Place in a preheated 350° oven. Cover and bake for 30 minutes. Serve hot, garnished with croutons and chopped parsley.

Creamed mussels

Mejillones a la crema

4 servings

- 32 large mussels, in their shells
- ½ teaspoon salt
  Freshly ground black pepper
- 1 cup dry white wine
- 4 tablespoons butter
- 1 cup sliced mushrooms
- 4 tablespoons flour
- 2 tablespoons brandy
  Juice of 1 lemon
- ¼ teaspoon grated nutmeg
- 1 cup heavy cream

Place the cleaned mussels in a saucepan with the salt, pepper and wine. Cover and cook for 7 minutes or until the shells open. Strain and reserve the liquid. Remove the mussels from their shells. Heat the butter, add the mushrooms and cook for 5 minutes. Stir in the flour and add the strained wine mixture from the mussels. Cook gently until thickened, stirring constantly. Add the brandy, lemon juice and nutmeg. Stir well and gradually pour in the cream. Add the mussels and reheat but do not boil.

Stuffed squid

Calamares rellenos

6 servings

- 12 squid
- 4 cups freshly made breadcrumbs
- ½ teaspoon salt
  Freshly ground black pepper
- ½ cup raisins
- ¼ cup grated Parmesan cheese
- 1 hard boiled egg, seived
- 2 anchovies, finely chopped
- 4 tablespoons melted butter
- 2 tablespoons oil
- 1 onion, finely chopped
- 6 tomatoes, peeled, seeded and chopped

Wash the squid. Cut off the tentacles and reserve a few for the stuffing. Discard the ink sack and the transparent cartilege from the back. Chop the reserved tentacles and place in a bowl. Add the breadcrumbs, salt, pepper, raisins, Parmesan cheese, hard boiled egg, anchovies and melted butter and combine thoroughly. Stuff the squid and arrange them in a buttered baking pan. Bake in a 350° oven 30 minutes. Meanwhile, heat the oil in a saucepan and sauté the onion until golden brown. Add the tomatoes and simmer 5 minutes. Pour the onion/tomato mixture over the squid and bake 15 minutes more.

Meat dishes

'Picadillo' is a name which covers
a whole range of dishes of cubed
or chopped meat mixed with
tomatoes, onions, olives, peppers,
nuts, raisins, fruits or whatever
happens to be on hand. It is served
alone as a main dish or used as a
stuffing for other dishes.

Stewed meat with onions and raisins—see recipe page 55

Stewed meat with onions and raisins

Picadillo

4 servings

> 2 pounds lean stewing beef,
>   cut into 1½ inch cubes
> 1 teaspoon salt
>   Water
> 2 tablespoons oil
> 1 onion, finely chopped
> 3 cloves garlic, crushed
> 3 large tomatoes, peeled,
>   seeded and chopped
> 1 red pepper, seeded and
>   chopped
> 12 pimiento stuffed olives
> ¼ teaspoon ground cloves
> 2 teaspoons vinegar
> ¾ cup raisins

Place the beef in a casserole. Add ½ teaspoon salt and water to barely cover the meat. Bring to a boil, lower the heat and simmer, covered, 1½ hours. Remove the cover and simmer until the liquid has almost completely evaporated. Heat the oil in a casserole and sauté the onion and garlic until golden brown. Add the tomatoes and simmer 5 minutes. Add the red pepper, olives, cloves and vinegar and simmer 10 to 15 minutes until the tomatoes are cooked to a purée. Add the beef and raisins and cook 10 minutes more, stirring frequently. Serve over rice.

In Peru, where meat is plentiful, luscious tidbits are marinated and spitted over hot coals for a special treat.

Barbecued meat

Barbecued meat

Anticuchos

4 servings

> 2 pounds sirloin steak, cut into
>   1 inch cubes
> 1 cup tarragon vinegar
> ½ cup water
> 2 fresh chili peppers, finely
>   chopped or
>   ½ teaspoon chili powder
> 2 cloves garlic, crushed
> ¼ teaspoon saffron
> 1 teaspoon salt
>   Freshly ground black pepper
> 3 tablespoons olive oil

Place the steak cubes in a bowl. Combine all the remaining ingredients and pour over the steak. Cover tightly with plastic wrap and refrigerate overnight, stirring occasionally. Thread the steak cubes on skewers and brush with olive oil. Broil 10 to 15 minutes until the meat reaches the desired degree of doneness. Turn frequently and baste with the marinade. Serve with corn on the cob or roasted sweet potatoes.

Though meat is plentiful in many countries of Latin America, it is almost never served without a carefully devised sauce. Even fine Argentinian beef is not as tender as the the corn-fed beef of the Middle Atlantic states, so good cooks have devised many ways to prepare meat to make it more tender and more interesting to eat. Meat may be larded with other fats; chopped into smaller pieces; marinated in tenderizing sauces; basted with spicy barbecue concoctions or preserved by smoking, pickling or salting. Pork is more common in Mexico than beef – and chicken even more plentiful. The great national fiesta dish of Mexico is turkey, prepared with an elaborate 'poblano' sauce which often has as many as twenty-five ingredients, including chocolate. (This sauce is now available in packaged form from Mexican speciality shops.) Throughout the Latin American countries meat is prepared with the addition of local vegetables – and sometimes fruits – but in a way which seldom occurs in North American cooking. The 'creole' stews use chunks of squash or pumpkin or coconut for thickening and sweetening. Peppers as well as oranges and lemons frequently add piquancy to simple dishes. The meat recipes of Latin America are of particular interest to the North American cook at It is wise to study them and apply the basic techniques to the less expensive cuts in the market today.

Meat balls 1

Albondigas

6 servings

2 pounds ground beef
½ cup chopped raisins
¼ cup chopped olives
1 teaspoon sugar
1 teaspoon salt
  Freshly ground black pepper
2 eggs, beaten
1 cup fine dry breadcrumbs
6 tablespoons butter
1 onion, chopped
1 clove garlic, crushed
2 tomatoes, peeled, seeded and
  chopped
1 tablespoon finely chopped
  parsley
½ cup beef broth

Combine the beef, raisins and olives. Season with the sugar, salt and pepper and mix well. Form into small balls and coat with egg and breadcrumbs. Heat the butter in a frying pan, add the onion and garlic and cook for 5 minutes. Add the meat balls and fry 15 minutes until brown and cooked. Add the tomatoes and simmer for 5 minutes. Remove the meat balls and keep them warm. Add the parsley and beef broth and simmer for 5 minutes. Pour the sauce over the meat balls and serve.

Meat balls with herbs

Albondigas con yerba buena

6 servings

1 pound ground lean beef
½ pound ground lean pork
1 cup cooked rice
1 large onion, finely chopped
1 clove garlic, crushed
1 tablespoon chopped fresh
  mint or 1 teaspoon dried mint
½ teaspoon sage
1 teaspoon salt
  Freshly ground black pepper
1 egg
3 hard boiled eggs, cut into
  small pieces
1 tablespoon oil
1 medium sized onion, finely
  chopped
2 cups tomato sauce
⅛ teaspoon ground coriander
¼ teaspoon salt
  Freshly ground black pepper
1 cup water

Place all the ingredients for the meatballs except the hard boiled eggs in a bowl and combine thoroughly. Shape the mixture into small balls, placing pieces of hard boiled egg in the center of each ball. Heat the oil in a casserole and sauté the onion until lightly browned. Add the tomato sauce, coriander, salt, pepper and water and bring to a simmer. Add the meatballs, cover and simmer 45 minutes. Serve from the casserole.

Garlic, onions and rice are mixed with finely chopped meat for Mexican meatballs ('albondigas') – then they are simmered in a savory tomato sauce.

Meat balls with herbs

Meat balls 2

Picadillo

4 servings

2 tablespoons olive oil
1 onion, finely chopped
1 pound ground lean beef
1 small clove garlic, crushed
2 tomatoes, peeled, seeded
  and chopped
1 tart green apple, peeled,
  cored and grated
¼ cup raisins, soaked in warm
  water and drained
2 tablespoons chopped
  black olives
3 tablespoons slivered
  almonds, toasted
1 egg
  Dash of cinnamon
  Dash of cloves
1 teaspoon chili powder
½ teaspoon salt
  Freshly ground black pepper
⅓ cup flour
3 tablespoons butter

Heat the olive oil in a small
skillet and sauté the onion until
golden brown. Drain off the oil
and transfer the onion to a
mixing bowl. Add the beef,
garlic, tomatoes, apple, raisins,
olives, almonds, egg, cinnamon,
cloves, chili powder, salt and
pepper and combine thoroughly.
Form the mixture into 8 balls
and dredge them in flour.
Heat the butter in a casserole
and sauté the meat balls until
lightly browned on all sides.
Lower the heat, cover the pan
and cook the meat balls slowly
20 minutes, turning them
occasionally. Serve with rice,
noodles or beans.

Meat balls in almond sauce

Albondigas en salsa de almendra

4 servings

1 cup almond sauce (recipe
  page 35)
1 cup beef broth
½ pound lean ground beef
½ pound lean ground pork
4 tablespoons fine dry
  breadcrumbs
1 egg
½ teaspoon nutmeg
1 teaspoon salt
  Freshly ground black pepper
4 tablespoons grated carrot
2 tablespoons finely chopped
  parsley

Combine the almond sauce and
beef broth and bring slowly to a
boil. Mix the beef, pork,
breadcrumbs, egg, nutmeg,
salt, pepper and grated carrot.
Form into walnut sized balls.
Add the meat balls to the
boiling sauce and simmer
gently 15 minutes until done.
Garnish with parsley. Serve the
meat balls in the sauce. These
may be served over rice. In
Mexico they are served with
hot tortillas.

Steak with Huancaina sauce

Lomo a la huancaina

6 servings

1 (3 ounce) package cream
  cheese
4 yolks of hard boiled eggs,
  sieved
2 fresh chili peppers, ground or
  ¾ teaspoon chili powder
¾ teaspoon salt
¼ cup olive oil
¾ cup heavy cream
1 tablespoon lemon juice
3 tablespoons finely chopped
  onion
6 individual steaks
12 ripe olives
3 hard boiled eggs, quartered

Beat the cheese until smooth.
Add the sieved egg yolks, chili
peppers and salt and beat with a
wooden spoon until smooth.
Add the olive oil a few drops at
a time, beating constantly. Add
the cream, lemon juice and
onion. Heat the mixture gently
in a saucepan but do not boil.
Broil the steaks to taste and
place on a serving platter. Pour
the sauce over the steaks and
garnish with olives and hard
boiled eggs.

Steak with peanut sauce

Cariucho

4 servings

2 tablespoons olive oil
1 onion, finely chopped
½ green pepper, seeded and
  chopped
2 tomatoes, peeled, seeded and
  chopped
¼ teaspoon chili powder
1 cup beef broth
½ cup ground unsalted peanuts
¼ cup heavy cream
3 tablespoons butter
4 individual steaks
½ teaspoon salt
  Freshly ground black pepper

Heat the olive oil in a saucepan
and sauté the onion and green
pepper 5 minutes over medium
heat. Add the tomatoes and
chili powder and simmer 5
minutes. Add the broth and
peanuts and simmer over very
low heat 25 to 30 minutes. Stir
in the cream gradually and bring
to simmering point. Keep the
sauce warm while preparing the
steaks. Heat the butter in a
large skillet and sauté the
steaks 3 minutes on each side or
until they reach the desired
degree of doneness. Sprinkle
them with salt and pepper and
arrange on a warm platter.
Pour the peanut sauce over the
steaks and serve immediately.

58

Rolled stuffed flank steak

Matambre

6 servings

1 (2½ pound) flank steak
1 teaspoon salt
Freshly ground black pepper
½ teaspoon thyme
¼ cup chopped parsley
1 onion, finely chopped
¼ cup wine vinegar

Filling:
½ pound spinach, washed and trimmed
1½ cups fresh, firm textured breadcrumbs
3 tablespoons milk
½ cup green peas
4 slices bacon, chopped and fried until crisp
¾ teaspoon salt
Freshly ground black pepper
4 carrots, cooked and sliced lengthwise
4 hard boiled eggs, quartered lengthwise
2 cups beef broth
1 cup water

Place the steak in a glass or earthenware dish. Sprinkle with salt, pepper, thyme, parsley, onion and vinegar. Cover and marinate overnight. To prepare the filling, spread the spinach leaves evenly over the steak. Mix the breadcrumbs with the milk. Add the peas, bacon, salt and pepper. Spread over the spinach leaves. Arrange the slices of carrots across the width of the steak, and place the eggs in rows in between. Roll the steak tightly and secure with strings tied 1 inch apart. Tie 2 pieces of string along the length of the steak. Place in a casserole and add the beef broth and water. Cover and place in a preheated 375° oven. Cook for 1¼ hours or until the steak is tender. Let rest for 10 minutes. Remove the strings. Cut into ¼ inch slices and serve hot, moistened with the pan juices. The beef may also be chilled and weighted with a heavy cooking utensil. It is then cut into thin slices and served cold.

Fillet of beef Mar del Plata

Lomo Mar del Plata

6 servings

3 tablespoons butter
3 pounds fillet of beef in 1 piece
2 yolks of hard boiled eggs, sieved
½ cup finely chopped mushrooms
2 tablespoons chopped parsley
2 tablespoons olive oil
¼ teaspoon salt
Freshly ground black pepper
4 slices bacon
1 cup dry white wine
½ cup beef broth
1 onion, chopped
1 bay leaf
¼ teaspoon thyme
3 peppercorns
2 tablespoons flour combined with 1 tablespoon softened butter

Heat the butter in a skillet and brown the beef quickly on all sides over high heat. Remove from the skillet. In a bowl, thoroughly combine the sieved egg yolks, mushrooms, parsley, olive oil, salt and pepper and spread the mixture over the beef. Wrap the bacon slices around the beef, and place in a roasting pan. Add the wine, broth, onion, bay leaf, thyme and peppercorns. Roast in a 350° oven 15 minutes. Turn and roast 10 minutes more. Transfer the beef to a heated platter and discard the bacon. Strain the liquid into a saucepan and add the flour mixture bit by bit, stirring constantly until the sauce thickens. Taste for seasoning and pour into a sauce boat. Slice the beef and serve beef and sauce separately.

'Matambre' translates literally as 'kill hunger' – which truly describes this wonderful beef roll, stuffed with vegetables and hard boiled eggs – a traditional dish served hot or cold in Argentina.

Rolled stuffed flank steak

Fried pastries with meat filling

Pasteis de carne

6 servings

Pastry:
- 3 cups flour
- 1 teaspoon salt
- 10 tablespoons shortening, melted to lukewarm
- ½ cup milk mixed with ½ cup hot water

Filling:
- 2 tablespoons oil
- 1 onion, chopped
- 1 clove garlic, crushed
- 2 tomatoes, peeled, seeded and chopped
- 1 pound ground beef
- ½ teaspoon salt
- 2 tablespoons finely chopped parsley
- 1 hard boiled egg, chopped
- ½ cup chopped mozzarella cheese
- 8 green olives, chopped
- Oil for deep frying

To prepare the pastry, sift the the flour and salt into a bowl. Add the melted shortening and warm milk and water. Mix to a smooth dough and cut into 2 pieces. To prepare the filling, heat the oil in a frying pan, add the onion and garlic and fry for 5 minutes until soft and golden. Add the tomatoes, ground beef and salt. Simmer for 20 minutes until almost dry. Remove from the heat. Add the chopped parsley, egg, cheese and olives and mix well. To assemble pastries, roll out the pastry on a floured board to ⅛ inch thickness. Cut 12 4-inch circles

from each piece. Place 1 tablespoon filling on each circle and moisten around the edge with water. Fold over and seal the edges well. Deep fry in preheated 375° oil for 4 to 5 minutes until golden and crisp. Remove with a slotted spoon and drain on absorbent paper. The pastries are also delicious cold and make good picnic fare. They may also be filled with ham, chicken or shrimp.

Beef creole

Bifes a la criolla

6 servings

- 3 tablespoons olive oil
- 2½ to 3 pounds sirloin, cut into ½ inch thick slices
- 4 potatoes, thickly sliced
- 4 tomatoes, peeled and thickly sliced
- 4 onions, thinly sliced
- 4 green peppers, seeded and cut into strips
- 2 tablespoons finely chopped parsley
- 1 teaspoon salt
  Freshly ground black pepper
- 1 cup beef broth
- 2 cloves garlic, crushed

Heat the oil in a skillet and sauté the sirloin slices over high heat until nicely browned. Remove from the skillet. In a large casserole, layer the meat, potatoes, tomatoes, onions and green peppers. Sprinkle the layers with parsley, salt and pepper. Pour the oil out of the skillet and add the beef broth and garlic. Bring to a simmer, scraping up the brown bits clinging to the pan. Pour over the meat and vegetables. Cover and simmer about 30 minutes until the potatoes are tender. Serve from the casserole with crusty bread and a green salad.

Pork and chicken

Piquete

6 to 8 servings

> 3 onions, chopped
> 2 cloves garlic, crushed
> 3 tablespoons chopped parsley
> 2 teaspoons salt
> ½ teaspoon chili powder
> 1 teaspoon ground cumin
> 1 (3½ pound) chicken, cut
>   into serving pieces
> 4 cups water
> 6 small potatoes, peeled
> 3 sweet potatoes, peeled and
>   halved
> 3 ears corn, cut in half
> 2 tablespoons butter
> 6 pork chops
> 1 teaspoon salt

Sauce:
> ½ cup breadcrumbs
> ¾ cup milk
> 4 tablespoons olive oil
> 2 onions, chopped
> 2 tomatoes, peeled, seeded
>   and chopped
> ½ cup grated Gruyère cheese
> 1 teaspoon salt

Combine the onions, garlic, parsley, salt, chili powder and cumin in a bowl. Pound together to form a paste. Coat the chicken pieces with this mixture. Cover and leave in the refrigerator overnight. Place the chicken/spice mixture and 4 cups water in a pan. Bring to a boil and simmer, covered, for 40 minutes. Remove the chicken and reserve the broth. Arrange the chicken pieces in a buttered baking pan and bake in a preheated 450° oven for 10 to 15 minutes until browned.

In the meantime, add the potatoes and sweet potatoes to the broth, bring to a boil and cook for 15 minutes. Add the corn and cook for 10 minutes longer. Heat the butter for frying the pork chops. Rub the pork chops with salt and fry until brown and tender. To prepare the sauce, soak the breadcrumbs in the milk. Heat the oil in a frying pan, add the onions and cook for 5 minutes until soft. Add the tomatoes and cook for 10 minutes, stirring frequently. Add the breadcrumbs and milk mixture and thin with additional milk if too thick. Add the grated cheese and salt and stir over low heat until the cheese melts. To serve, arrange the chicken and pork chops on a heated platter and the potatoes and corn on another platter. Serve the sauce separately in a sauce boat.

Pickled and fried spareribs

Costillas de cerdo en vinagre

4 servings

> 1 cup vinegar
> 2 teaspoons salt
>   Freshly ground black pepper
> 1 teaspoon paprika
> ½ teaspoon marjoram
> 3 pounds spareribs, cut into
>   single ribs
> 5 eggs
> 2 tablespoons flour
> ½ cup fine dry breadcrumbs
> 2 tablespoons finely chopped
>   parsley
>   Oil for deep frying

In a shallow pan, combine the vinegar, 1 teaspoon salt, pepper, paprika and marjoram. Add the ribs, turning to coat them on all sides. Let the ribs marinate 2 hours at room temperature, turning them occasionally. Remove the ribs from the marinade and roast in a 400° oven 10 minutes. Let them cool 20 minutes. Beat together the eggs, remaining salt, flour, breadcrumbs and parsley. Heat the oil for deep frying. Dip each rib in the batter and deep fry about 10 minutes until golden brown. Drain on paper towels and serve immediately.

Pepper pork

Aji de carne

6 servings

> 6 tablespoons olive oil
> 3 onions, chopped
> 3 cloves garlic, crushed
> 3 tablespoons rice
> 2½ pounds pork, cut into ½ inch
>   cubes
> 4 tomatoes, peeled, seeded and
>   chopped
> ¼ teaspoon saffron
> 1 teaspoon salt
>   Freshly ground black pepper
> ¼ teaspoon chili powder
> 1 whole clove
> ¼ teaspoon cinnamon
> 2 cups beef broth
> 4 potatoes, peeled and
>   quartered
> 2 green bananas, peeled and
>   quartered
> ½ cup ground unsalted peanuts
> ½ cup heavy cream
> 1 tablespoon molasses

Heat the oil in a large saucepan. Add the onions and garlic and fry for 5 minutes, stirring frequently. Add the rice and pork and fry over high heat until the meat is brown. Add the tomatoes, saffron, salt, pepper, chili powder, clove, cinnamon and beef broth. Cover and cook over low heat for 30 minutes. Add the potatoes and bananas and cook for 25 minutes longer. Stir in the peanuts, cream and molasses and continue cooking until heated through. Serve hot.

Creole stew

Boiled meat

Pork stew with vegetables and fruit

Carbonada Criolla

6 servings

    1 (8 to 10 pound) pumpkin
    2 tablespoons butter, melted
 1½ teaspoons salt
    Freshly ground black pepper

Filling:
    3 tablespoons butter
    2 pounds chuck steak, cut into
       1 inch cubes
    1 large onion, chopped
    1 clove garlic, crushed
    1 teaspoon salt
       Freshly ground black pepper
    1 teaspoon sugar
    2 tomatoes, peeled, seeded and
       coarsely chopped
 1½ cups beef broth
    3 white potatoes, peeled and
       cut into ½ inch cubes
    2 cups frozen or canned corn
    4 peaches, peeled, halved and
       pitted

Wash the pumpkin and cut a
circle 6 inches in diameter from
the top. Remove the seeds.
Brush the inside with melted
butter and sprinkle with salt
and pepper. Bake in a preheated
375° oven for 45 minutes until
tender but firm when pierced
with a fork. To prepare the
filling, heat the butter, add the
beef and fry until brown on all
sides. Remove the meat, add the
onion and garlic and fry for
5 minutes until soft. Return the
meat to the pan and add the
salt, pepper, sugar, tomatoes
and broth. Bring to a boil,
cover and cook for 25 minutes.
Add the potatoes and continue
cooking for 15 minutes. Add the
corn and peaches and continue
cooking for 5 minutes. Spoon the
mixture into the baked
pumpkin, replace the lid and
bake for another 15 minutes in a
preheated 375° oven. Place the
pumpkin on a large serving
platter and ladle the carbonada
from the pumpkin to serve.

Puchero criollo

6 servings

    1 cup dried chick peas or
       Great Northern beans
    8 cups water
    2 pounds short ribs of beef
 ½ pound lean salt pork, sliced
 3½ pounds chicken, cut into
       pieces
 1½ teaspoons salt
       Freshly ground black pepper
    3 spicy sausages (Spanish if
       possible), sliced
    4 carrots, sliced
    4 onions
    3 cloves garlic, crushed
    1 small zucchini, peeled and
       sliced
    4 tomatoes
    1 small cabbage, cut into
       eighths
    1 green pepper, seeded and
       chopped
    4 potatoes, peeled and sliced
    2 leeks, cut into rings
    2 tablespoons chopped parsley

Cover the dried peas with water
and soak overnight. Drain.
Measure 8 cups water into a
large saucepan and add the
chick peas. (If canned chick peas
are used, do not add them until
the last 20 minutes.) Bring the
water to a boil, add the beef,
pork, chicken, salt and pepper.
Cover, reduce heat and simmer
for 1¼ hours. Add the sausages
and carrots and cook for 15
minutes. Add the onions, garlic,
zucchini, tomatoes, cabbage,
green pepper, potatoes, leeks
and parsley. Cook for 20 minutes
or until the potatoes are tender.
Correct the seasoning. Remove
the meats and arrange on a hot
platter. Place the vegetables
around the meat and serve hot.

Estofado de cerdo

6 servings

    2 pounds lean pork, cubed
 1½ cups water
    1 bay leaf
    2 cloves
 ¼ teaspoon thyme
    1 teaspoon salt
    1 cup green chili pepper
       sauce (recipe page 34)
    4 tablespoons ground almonds
    2 ripe pears, peeled, seeded
       and sliced
    2 bananas, peeled and sliced
    2 small ripe apples, peeled,
       cored and sliced
    4 thin slices mango, peeled
    2 medium sized zucchini, peeled
       and sliced lengthwise
 ½ cup cooked green peas
 ½ cup canned corn

Place the pork, water, bay leaf,
cloves, thyme and salt in a
saucepan. Bring to a boil,
reduce the heat, cover and
simmer gently for 30 minutes.
Drain the pork. Strain and
reserve the cooking broth.
Add the green sauce to the
almonds and add to the strained
cooking liquid from the meat.
Arrange layers of meat, fruit
and zucchini in a deep casserole.
Pour over the sauce. Cover
and cook for another 25 minutes.
Do not stir. Mix the green peas
with the corn. Arrange on top
of the stew. Cover and
continue cooking for 5 minutes.

*Argentina is famous for its beef
and its cooks have devised
wonderful ways to make the often
tough, range-fed meat tender and*
*tasty. Here it is simmered with
salt pork, sausage, chicken and an
array of garden fresh vegetables*

Boiled meat

Brazil's great national dish combines a variety of preserved meats with black beans to make a 'feijoada completa'
The traditional Feijoada uses 15 meats but not all are readily available. Your Feijoada will be
excellent using just the meats called for in this recipe.

Brazilian stew — see recipe page 63

Brazilian stew

Feijoada completa

10 to 12 servings

1 smoked beef tongue
2 pounds black beans, soaked
   overnight and drained
2 pounds carne seca (dried
   beef), soaked overnight and
   drained
2 pounds linguica (seasoned
   Brazilian pork sausage)
½ pound bacon, in 1 piece
½ pound smoked loin of pork
½ pound salt pork, cubed
2 tablespoons oil
2 onions, finely chopped
2 cloves garlic, crushed
2 tomatoes, peeled, seeded and
   chopped
2 bay leaves
2 tablespoons finely chopped
   parsley
4 oranges, peeled and sliced

Place the tongue in a large pan and add water to cover. Bring to a boil, lower the heat and simmer, covered, 2½ hours until tender. Drain and remove the skin and any gristle when the tongue is cool enough to handle. Place the beans, carne seca, linguica, bacon, pork loin and salt pork in a very large casserole. Add cold water to cover. Bring to a boil, lower the heat and simmer, covered, 1 hour. Check occasionally to see if the liquid is being absorbed too quickly by the beans. Add boiling water as necessary to keep the ingredients barely covered. Add the tongue and continue cooking 1 hour until the beans are tender. Heat the oil in a skillet and sauté the onions and garlic until soft. Add the tomatoes, bay leaves and parsley and simmer 5 minutes. Remove about 2 cups of the black beans from the casserole with a slotted spoon and mash them into the onion/tomato mixture. Cook, stirring constantly, about 2 minutes.

Remove and slice the meats. Arrange them on a large platter with the tongue in the center. Garnish with orange slices. Add the thick bean sauce to the remaining black beans in the casserole. Cook, stirring, about 2 minutes. Place the beans in a soup tureen. Serve the Feijoada with rice, couve miniera and a hot pepper sauce.

Rice:

3 tablespoons oil
1 onion, finely chopped
1 clove garlic, crushed
3 tomatoes, peeled, seeded and
   chopped
3 cups rice
½ teaspoon salt
   Freshly ground black pepper
6 cups boiling water

Heat the oil in a saucepan and sauté the onion and garlic until soft. Add the tomatoes and simmer 10 minutes. Add the rice, salt, pepper and boiling water and stir once with a fork. Lower the heat, cover and simmer 30 minutes until the rice has absorbed all the liquid.

Couve miniera (spring greens):

1 head Boston lettuce
2 pounds fresh spinach
1 pound endive lettuce
   (You may substitute 4
   pounds other spring greens
   for the above)
3 slices bacon, chopped
1 clove garlic, crushed
¼ teaspoon salt

Wash the greens and cut off the stalks. Stack several leaves of various greens, one on top of the other and roll up. Slice very thinly. Cook in boiling water a few seconds and drain. Squeeze out all the water. Fry the bacon in a skillet until the fat has rendered. Add the garlic and greens and sauté over medium heat for 2 minutes, stirring constantly. Season with salt.

Leg of lamb Mexican style

Pierna de carnero a la mexicana

8 servings

2 tablespoons softened butter
2 cloves garlic, crushed
1 tablespoon oregano
1 teaspoon crushed caraway
   seeds
1 teaspoon chili powder
1½ teaspoons brown sugar
1 teaspoon salt
1 (4 to 5 pound) leg of lamb
¼ cup red wine vinegar
½ cup olive oil
1 onion, sliced into rings

Beat the butter until creamy. Add the garlic, oregano, caraway seeds, chili powder, brown sugar and salt and combine thoroughly. With a sharp knife, make incisions all over the leg of lamb and stuff each incision with a little of the butter mixture. Combine the vinegar, olive oil and onion in a large pan. Add the lamb, turning it to coat with the marinade. Cover and refrigerate 36 hours. Turn the lamb and baste with the marinade frequently. Remove the lamb from the refrigerator 2 hours before you plan to roast it. Wipe off the excess marinade with paper towels. Place the lamb on a rack in a roasting pan and roast in a 350° oven 1½ hours for medium rare or 2 hours for well done. Serve with baked potatoes.

Spiced loin of pork

Lomo de cerdo adobado

4 servings

1 tablespoon chili powder
2 tablespoons flour
2 tablespoons wine vinegar
1 teaspoon salt
8 caraway seeds, crushed
3 cloves garlic, crushed
1 pound boneless pork loin,
   cut into ½ inch strips
¼ cup flour
4 tablespoons butter or olive oil
1 head of lettuce, shredded
2 medium sized onions, cut
   into paper thin rings

Combine the chili powder, flour, vinegar, salt, caraway seeds and garlic. Add enough water to make a coating consistency. Marinate the pork in this mixture for 30 minutes. The longer the meat marinates, the sharper the taste will be. Remove the pork from the chili paste and dredge with flour. Heat the butter or oil and brown the pork strips over high heat on all sides. Serve on a bed of shredded lettuce and garnish with paper thin onion rings.

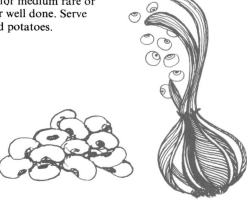

Mexico's spicy meat pie uses four
kinds of meat and is laced with a
generous splash of sherry.

Spicy meat pie

La olla con carne

6 servings

Pastry:
2½ cups flour
¾ teaspoon salt
½ teaspoon baking powder
6 tablespoons butter, cut into
   small pieces
6 tablespoons margarine
8 tablespoons cold water

Filling:
½ pound pork, cubed
½ pound veal, cubed
½ pound beef, cubed
½ pound boneless chicken,
   cubed
1½ teaspoons salt
   Freshly ground black pepper
⅛ teaspoon nutmeg
⅛ teaspoon cinnamon
4 tablespoons flour
¼ cup water
½ cup sherry

To prepare the pastry, sift the
flour, salt and baking powder
into a bowl. Add the butter and
blend into the flour with the
fingertips until the size of small
peas. Mix in the margarine. Stir
in the cold water with a fork,
adding 4 tablespoons first, then
1 tablespoon at a time. Chill for
20 minutes. Cut the pastry in
half and roll on a lightly floured
board. Fit the pastry into a 9
inch pie pan. Mix the meats,
seasonings and flour. Fill the
pastry with the meat. Add the
water and ½ the sherry. Cover
with the second round of pastry.
Cut a 2 inch slit in the center.
Bake in a 350° oven 2 hours.
Pour remaining sherry through
the slit in the top crust
before serving.

Peppered chicken

Aji de gallina

4 servings

        1 (3 pound) chicken
        4 cups water
        1 onion
        1 carrot
        1 tomato
        1 teaspoon salt
           Freshly ground black pepper
    ¼ cup olive oil
        1 onion, finely chopped
        1 clove garlic, crushed
    ½ teaspoon cumin seed
        2 cups firm textured fresh
           breadcrumbs
    ½ to 1 teaspoon red hot pepper
           sauce
    ½ cup grated Parmesan cheese
        4 potatoes, peeled, cut into
           1 inch cubes and boiled
        4 ears corn on the cob, cooked
        4 hard boiled eggs, quartered

Place the chicken, water, onion,
carrot, tomato, salt and pepper
in a large saucepan. Bring to
boiling point. Reduce the heat,
cover and simmer for 1 hour
until the chicken is tender. Drain
and reserve the broth. Remove
the chicken from the bones and
shred finely. Heat the oil, add
the onion, garlic and cumin seed
and fry for 5 minutes until soft
and golden. Add the
breadcrumbs, pepper sauce,
cheese and 2 cups of the
reserved chicken broth. Simmer
gently for 10 minutes. Add the
shredded chicken and thin with
additional chicken broth if
necessary. Serve with boiled
potatoes and corn on the cob.
Garnish with hard boiled eggs.

*Peruvians prefer chicken in a red
pepper sauce, flavored with
onions, garlic and tomatoes, and
garnished with hard boiled eggs.*

Chicken in orange juice and pineapple

Pollo en jugo de naranja y pina

4 servings

½ cup raisins
1 cup orange juice
1 (3½ pound) chicken, cut into serving pieces
½ cup flour seasoned with 1 teaspoon salt and Freshly ground black pepper
3 tablespoons oil
½ cup chopped blanched almonds
½ cup crushed pineapple, drained
2 tablespoons sugar
¼ teaspoon cinnamon
⅛ teaspoon ground cloves

Soak the raisins in the orange juice 2 to 3 hours. Dredge the chicken pieces in seasoned flour. Heat the oil in a skillet and sauté the chicken until golden brown on all sides. Transfer to a shallow baking dish. Add the remaining ingredients to the raisins and orange juice and spoon the mixture over the chicken. Bake in a 325° oven 30 minutes, basting frequently. Raise the heat to 400° and continue cooking 10 minutes. Serve immediately.

Chicken with mushrooms

Galinja di champignons

4 servings

1 (2 to 3 pound) chicken
2 cups water
½ teaspoon salt
Freshly ground black pepper
2 tablespoons butter
2 tablespoons flour
1 teaspoon curry powder
1 cup milk
1 (16 ounce) can sliced mushrooms
½ cup grated Mozzarella or Muenster cheese
4 eggs, beaten
¼ teaspoon salt
½ cup breadcrumbs

Place the chicken in a large saucepan. Add the water, salt and pepper. Bring to a boil, reduce the heat, cover and simmer gently for 1 hour until tender. Bone and skin the chicken and cut into small pieces. Heat the butter in a saucepan. Stir in the flour and curry powder and cook for 2 minutes. Gradually add the milk, stirring constantly, and cook until the sauce has thickened. If necessary, add chicken broth if the sauce is too thick. Butter an ovenproof dish. Cover with a layer of chicken. Pour the sauce over, cover with sliced mushrooms and cheese. Add the beaten eggs and salt and sprinkle with breadcrumbs. Bake in a preheated 350° oven for 20 to 25 minutes until the top is firm and brown.

Fried chicken

Chicarrones de pollo

4 servings

¼ cup soy sauce
¼ cup lemon juice
¼ cup dark rum
1 (2½ to 3 pound) chicken, cut into serving pieces
½ cup flour
1 teaspoon salt
Freshly ground black pepper
½ cup olive oil

Combine the soy sauce, lemon juice and rum. Pour over the chicken and marinate for 2 hours, basting occasionally. Mix the flour, salt and pepper. Dredge the chicken in seasoned flour. Heat the oil and fry the the pieces of chicken 30 to 35 minutes until tender and brown. Serve with rice and a crisp green salad.

Chicken livers in sauce

Higra stoba

4 servings

- 3 tablespoons oil
- 2 onions, finely chopped
- 2 cloves garlic, crushed
- 2 green peppers, seeded and cut into strips
- 1 pound chicken livers, washed and dried
- 5 tablespoons soy sauce
- 1 tablespoon sugar

Heat the oil in a large skillet and sauté the onions, garlic and green peppers for 4 minutes, stirring constantly. Add the chicken livers, soy sauce and sugar and cook, stirring, 5 minutes. Serve over rice.

In Puerto Rico, chicken and rice are cooked together with fresh tomatoes in the perfect blending of taste and nutrition.

Squabs stuffed with noodles

Pollita de grano

6 servings

- 1 pair sweetbreads
- 1 cup water
- 1 tablespoon vinegar
- 2 teaspoons salt
  Freshly ground black pepper
- 2 cloves garlic, crushed
- 6 squabs or Cornish hens, livers reserved
- 6 tablespoons butter
- 1 onion, finely chopped
- 1 cup finely chopped mushrooms
- 2 cups medium fine egg noodles, cooked and drained
- ⅔ cup heavy cream
- ⅓ cup dry sherry

Wash the sweetbreads in cold water and place them in a saucepan. Add the water and vinegar. Bring to a boil, lower the heat and simmer 10 minutes. Drain, cover with cold water and set aside 20 minutes. Drain off the water, peel the membrane from the sweetbreads and chop them into small cubes. Combine 1 teaspoon salt, pepper and garlic in a small bowl and rub the mixture into the cavities of the squabs. Chop the livers and set aside. Heat 3 tablespoons of the butter in a skillet and sauté the onion until softened. Add the mushrooms and livers and sauté 2 or 3 minutes more. Add the noodles, sweetbreads, cream, sherry, remaining salt and pepper and combine thoroughly. Stuff the squabs with the mixture and secure the openings with skewers. Heat the remaining butter in a large casserole or baking pan and sauté the squabs over high heat until nicely browned on all sides. Bake in a 375° oven 35 minutes, basting frequently with the butter. Place the squabs on a heated platter, remove the skewers and serve immediately.

Rice with chicken

Asapao

4 servings

- 2 cloves garlic, crushed
- 1 teaspoon oregano
- 1 teaspoon salt
- 1 chicken, cut into serving pieces
- 4 strips bacon, cut up
- 2 tablespoons butter
- 1 onion, chopped
- ½ cup diced cooked ham
- 4 tomatoes, peeled, seeded and sliced
- 3 cups chicken broth
- 1 cup raw rice
- 1 package frozen green peas, cooked
- 4 tablespoons grated Parmesan cheese
- 1 tablespoon capers
- 1 sweet red pepper, seeded and cut into strips

Combine the garlic, oregano and salt and rub the chicken pieces with this mixture. Fry the bacon in a deep frying pan. Add the butter and brown the chicken on all sides over high heat. Remove the chicken from the pan. Add the onion and fry for 5 minutes until soft and golden. Add the ham and tomatoes and cook for 10 minutes. Return the chicken to the pan with 1 cup chicken broth and simmer over low heat for 30 minutes. Remove the chicken. Add the rice and remaining broth to the sauce and stir well. Bring to a boil, reduce heat, cover and simmer for 25 minutes or until the rice is tender. Bone the chicken and cut the meat into small pieces. Add chicken, green peas, cheese and capers to the rice and blend well. Arrange pepper strips on top. Cover the pan and simmer over low heat for 5 minutes. Serve from the pan.

Rice with chicken

*Chicken is simmered in a savory
vinegar sauce with red peppers,
garlic, lemon, bay leaf and
parsley for a real taste sensation
in Venezuela*

Venezuelan chicken with vinegar—see recipe page 69

Venezuelan chicken in vinegar

Pollo em vinagre

4 servings

- 1 (3 pound) chicken, cut into serving pieces
- ½ cup flour seasoned with 1 teaspoon salt
- 6 tablespoons oil
- 2 tomatoes, peeled, seeded and chopped
- 1 red or green pepper, seeded and cut into strips
- 4 cloves garlic, crushed
- 1 (4 ounce) can mushrooms
- 1 can artichoke hearts
- 2 tablespoons vinegar
- 1 bay leaf
  Juice of 1 lemon
- 1 tablespoon chopped parsley
- ½ cup red wine
- ½ teaspoon salt
  Freshly ground black pepper

Dredge the chicken pieces in seasoned flour. Heat 4 tablespoons of the oil in a frying pan. Add the chicken and fry over high heat until well browned. Transfer the chicken to a casserole. Add tomatoes, red or green pepper, garlic and 1 cup juice from canned mushrooms and artichokes. (If necessary, add water to make 1 cup.) Add remaining oil, vinegar and bay leaf and simmer for 10 minutes. Add lemon juice, parsley, wine, salt and pepper. Simmer for 20 minutes until all the ingredients are well blended and the chicken is tender. Add the mushrooms and artichoke hearts and heat thoroughly. Serve with rice.

'Shrimps and rice are very nice' – especially when combined with chicken and flavored with cumin and coriander as they are in the Guyanas.

Chicken, shrimp and rice

Chicken, shrimp and rice

Pollo con arroz

6 to 8 servings

- 1 (4 pound) chicken
- 7 cups water
- 2 leeks, sliced
- 1 bay leaf
- 2 sprigs parsley
- 1 tablespoon salt
- 8 peppercorns
- 1½ cups rice
- 4 tablespoons peanut oil
- 2 medium sized onions, finely chopped
- 2 cloves garlic, crushed
- 1½ cups chopped cooked shrimp
- 1 cup crabmeat
- 1 cup chopped ham
- 2 teaspoons ground coriander
- 1 teaspoon ground cumin
- ½ teaspoon chili powder
- ¼ teaspoon mace
- ½ cup chopped unsalted peanuts

Place the chicken, water, leeks, bay leaf, parsley, salt and peppercorns in a large pot and bring to a boil. Lower the heat, cover, and simmer 1¼ hours until the chicken is tender. Remove the chicken and let cool. Strain and reserve the broth. Remove the skin from the chicken and slice the meat into strips. Bring 3 cups of the reserved broth to a boil. Add the rice and stir once with a fork. Lower the heat, cover and cook the rice about 25 minutes or until all the liquid is absorbed. Heat the oil in a large, heavy casserole and sauté the onions and garlic until golden brown. Add the rice and cook until lightly browned, stirring frequently. Add the chicken, shrimp, crabmeat, ham, coriander, cumin, chili powder, mace and about ¼ cup broth and combine thoroughly. Cook over low heat about 10 minutes or until the ingredients are heated through. Stir frequently. Stir in the peanuts and serve immediately.

Chicken in pepper sauce

Aji de pollo

6 to 8 servings

    6   tablespoons olive oil
    2   (3½ pound) chickens, cut
        into serving pieces
    2   onions, thinly sliced
    2   cloves garlic, crushed
    1   teaspoon salt
        Freshly ground black pepper
    2   cups chicken broth
    2   onions, finely chopped
  1½   cups canned Italian style
        tomatoes
    4   small potatoes, peeled and
        diced
    1   red or green pepper, seeded
        and cut into thin strips
    ½   teaspoon chili powder
    ½   teaspoon marjoram
    1   cup freshly made
        breadcrumbs
    4   hard boiled eggs, quartered
   12   pitted black olives

Heat 4 tablespoons oil in a large casserole and sauté the chicken pieces until nicely browned on all sides. Remove from the pan and keep warm. Sauté the sliced onions and garlic in the same oil until brown. Pour off all the oil. Return the chicken to the pan and add ½ teaspoon salt, pepper and 1 cup broth. Bring to a boil, lower the heat and simmer, covered, 45 minutes to 1 hour or until the chicken is tender. Meanwhile, heat the remaining oil in a saucepan and sauté the chopped onions until softened. Add the tomatoes, potatoes, red or green pepper, chili powder, marjoram and remaining salt. Simmer vigorously 5 minutes, stirring constantly. Add the remaining broth, cover and cook slowly 20 minutes. Stir in the breadcrumbs and add the tomato mixture to the chicken cooking liquid. Bring to a simmer, stirring, and taste for seasoning. Garnish with hard boiled eggs and olives and serve immediately.

Chicken and rice

Pollo pilau

6 servings

    2   (2½ to 3 pound) chickens,
        cut into serving pieces
    1   teaspoon salt
  1½   cups rice
    1   cup raisins
    ½   cup light cream
    3   tablespoons melted butter
    ¼   teaspoon nutmeg

Place the chicken pieces in a casserole and add the salt and water to cover. Bring to a simmer and stir in the rice. Cover and cook over the lowest possible heat 30 minutes. Stir in the raisins and cook, covered, 15 minutes more until the chicken is just tender. Arrange the chicken pieces on a heated serving platter. Drain any liquid from the rice. Add the light cream, butter and nutmeg and combine thoroughly. Pack the rice firmly into cups or molds and invert onto the serving platter around the chicken. Serve immediately.

Chicken hunter's style

Pollo al cazador

6 servings

    ¼   cup dried chick peas
    1   teaspoon salt
        Freshly ground black pepper
    ¼   cup flour
    2   (3 pound) chickens, cut into
        serving pieces
    ⅓   cup olive oil
    3   onions, quartered
    3   tomatoes, peeled, seeded and
        chopped
  1½   cups sliced mushrooms
    2   green peppers, sliced
  1½   cups red wine
    ¼   teaspoon chili powder
    ¼   teaspoon oregano
    1   bay leaf

Wash and soak the chick peas in water overnight. Drain well. Cover with boiling water and simmer for 1½ hours or until tender. Drain. Combine the salt, pepper and flour and coat the chicken pieces. Heat the olive oil in a heavy saucepan. Add the chicken and fry over moderately high heat for 10 minutes until lightly browned. Add the chick peas, onions, tomatoes, mushrooms, green peppers, wine, chili powder, oregano and bay leaf. Cover and cook over low heat for 1 hour or until the chicken is tender. Remove the bay leaf and serve.

Chicken in nut sauce

Pollo en nogado

4 servings

Sauce:
- *1 cup chopped mixed nuts*
- *½ onion, chopped*
- *1 slice stale white bread, crumbled*
- *½ cup milk*
- *2 cloves garlic, crushed*
- *¼ teaspoon ground cloves*
- *¼ teaspoon cinnamon*
- *1 teaspoon chili powder or 1 green fresh chili, peeled, seeded and chopped*
- *1 tablespoon tomato paste*
- *½ teaspoon salt*

- *6 tablespoons butter*
- *1 (3 pound) chicken, cut into serving pieces*
- *1 teaspoon salt*
- *1 cup water*

To prepare the sauce, combine the ingredients in an electric blender and blend for 30 seconds until a smooth purée is formed. Heat 2 tablespoons butter in a frying pan, add the purée and cook over low heat for 5 minutes. Dry the chicken and sprinkle with salt. Heat 4 tablespoons butter and brown the chicken on all sides over high heat. Add 1 cup water and bring to a boil. Reduce the heat and simmer for 30 minutes. Drain the chicken and add ½ the puréed sauce. Return the chicken to the pan and cook, uncovered, over low heat for 10 minutes, basting with the sauce. Transfer to a heated serving dish and pour the remaining sauce over the chicken.

Turkey in green sauce

Pavo en salsa verde

4 servings

- *¼ cup pepitas (pumpkin seeds)*
- *½ cup blanched and chopped almonds and English walnuts*
- *1 fresh or canned chili poblano, peeled, seeded and finely chopped*
- *1 green pepper, seeded and finely chopped*
- *1 (10 ounce) can Mexican green tomatoes, chopped*
- *1 onion, chopped*
- *2 tablespoons coarsely chopped coriander or parsley*
- *½ clove garlic, crushed*
- *1 cup chicken or turkey broth*
- *½ teaspoon salt*
- *2 tablespoons olive oil*
- *2 to 3 pounds cooked turkey, cut into pieces*
- *2 tablespoons parsley, finely chopped*

Combine the pepitas, almonds, walnuts, chili poblano, green pepper, tomatoes, onion, coriander or parsley, garlic and broth in an electric blender to form a smooth purée. Season to taste with salt. Heat the olive oil in a saucepan and gradually stir in the green sauce. Add the pieces of turkey and simmer for 15 minutes. Garnish with chopped parsley and serve with hot tortillas (recipe page 37).

Turkey casserole

Cacerola de pavo

6 to 8 servings

- *1 (8 pound) turkey, cut into serving pieces*
- *2 teaspoons salt*
  Freshly ground black pepper
- *1 teaspoon paprika*
- *3 cloves garlic, crushed*
- *¾ cup vinegar*
- *2 bay leaves*
- *¼ cup olive oil*
- *3 tablespoons butter*
- *2 onions, chopped*
- *2 cups chicken broth*
- *2 green peppers, sliced*
- *12 green olives, sliced*
- *½ cup capers, drained*

Place the turkey pieces in a shallow glass or earthenware bowl. Mix together the salt, pepper, paprika and garlic. Rub into the turkey pieces. Add the vinegar and bay leaves. Marinate for 2 hours. Drain. Heat the olive oil and butter in a heavy saucepan. Add the turkey and onions and cook over high heat until the turkey is well browned on all sides. Add the chicken broth. Cover and cook over low heat for 1¾ hours or until the turkey is tender. Add the green peppers, olives and capers and cook for 10 minutes. Correct the seasoning. Serve immediately.

Turkey in chocolate sauce

Pavo en mole poblano

6 to 8 servings

- *1 (6 pound) turkey or roasting chicken, cut into serving pieces*
- *1 teaspoon salt*
- *½ cup flour*
- *½ cup lard*
- *2 cups spicy chocolate sauce (recipe page 36)*
- *4 teaspoons toasted sesame seeds*

Place the turkey pieces in a large pan. Add the salt and water to cover. Bring to a boil, lower the heat and simmer, covered, 1 hour or until barely tender. Strain the broth and use for the chocolate sauce (see page 36) instead of chicken broth. Dry the turkey pieces on paper towels and dredge in flour. Heat the lard in a large skillet and sauté the turkey until golden brown on all sides. Transfer the turkey to a casserole and add the chocolate sauce. Cover and simmer 20 minutes. Sprinkle with sesame seeds and serve immediately.

It is sometimes said that Latin America is basically a 'corn culture.' This was probably true in very primitive times, but it seems a dreadful understatement when one thinks of the marvels which the Indians and then later the Europeans have done with the careful cultivation and preparation not only of corn, but of beans and rice and other vegetables also.

The early Indians discovered that they could plant beans and corn in a rotation which preserved the quality of the soil as well as the balance of the diet. But it is a mistake to think of the Latin Americans in terms of beans and corn – even though these two vegetables are so important. Tomatoes, potatoes, all the members of the squash family, have been in everyday use since the most ancient times. The Spaniards added garlic and onions, and the basic 'sofrito', a gentle melding of garlic, onions and tomatoes has become the base of many, many dishes throughout the continent. The hot peppers which add such piquancy to food are rich in vitamins A and C – and the custom of blending several kinds of vegetables in a single dish offers not only a variety of taste sensations, but excellent nutrition as well. Beans come in a dozen varieties throughout the region. Mexico offers its 'frijoles refritos' (fried beans) as an essential ingredient of every meal. Brazil's national dish; 'feijoada completa', is based on black beans. Garbanzos are used in as many dishes as are lentils and they are both filling and nutritious. Did you know, by the way, that a dish of chili con carne has fewer calories than an equal dish of just plain meat? The beans provide the same protein with fewer calories.

Potatoes with cheese and onion sauce

Huancaina papas

4 servings

- 6 potatoes, peeled, boiled and diced
- 2 tablespoons butter
- 1 large onion, finely chopped
- 1 cup cottage cheese
- ½ cup milk
- 1 teaspoon lemon juice
- ½ teaspoon salt
  Freshly ground black pepper
- 1 teaspoon paprika

Chill the cooked potatoes. Heat the butter in a frying pan. Add the onion and fry for 5 minutes until soft. Remove from the heat and add the cottage cheese, milk, lemon juice, salt, pepper and paprika. Beat well until smooth. Serve this sauce over the potatoes. This dish is served cold.

Refried beans

Frijoles refritos

4 to 6 servings

- 2 cups pinto or kidney beans
- 2 large onions, chopped
- 2 large tomatoes, peeled, seeded and chopped
- 1 clove garlic, crushed
- 1 canned hot chili pepper, minced
- 1 teaspoon salt
  Freshly ground black pepper
- ½ cup lard
- 2 tablespoons flour

Soak the beans overnight in water to cover. Drain and add fresh cold water to cover. Add the onions, tomatoes, garlic, chili pepper, salt and black pepper. Bring to a boil, lower the heat and simmer 2 or 3 hours until the beans are soft. As the water evaporates, add more boiling water to keep the ingredients barely covered. Drain off the excess water and mash the beans with a potato masher. Heat the lard in a large skillet. Add the flour and cook, stirring, until it begins to brown. Add the bean mixture and cook, stirring, until the lard is completely absorbed and the beans are fairly dry. Mold into a long roll on a heated serving plate and serve with tortillas (recipe page 37), fried until crisp.

Refried beans

Mexico's famous 'refried beans' aren't really refried at all. This famous dish appears on Mexican tables at every meal from breakfast to midnight snacks.

Brown beans with rice

BB met R

4 servings

    3 tablespoons butter
 1½ to 2 pounds stewing beef,
    cut into 1½ inch cubes
    1 onion, chopped
    2 cloves garlic, crushed
    2 tomatoes, peeled, seeded
    and chopped
    1 to 2 cups beef broth
    1 bay leaf
  ½ teaspoon salt
    Freshly ground black pepper
    1 (16 ounce) can kidney
    beans, drained
    3 cups cooked rice

Heat the butter in a casserole
and sauté the beef cubes over
high heat until nicely browned
on all sides. Lower the heat,
add the onion and garlic and
sauté 5 minutes. Add the
tomatoes and cook 5 minutes
more. Add 1 cup broth, the
bay leaf, salt and pepper and
bring to a boil. Lower the heat,
cover and simmer 1½ to 2
hours until the beef is tender.
If the meat becomes too dry,
add a few tablespoons more
broth from time to time. The
mixture should be quite thick.
Stir in the beans, cover and
simmer 15 minutes more. Place
the rice on a heated platter
and spoon the meat mixture on
top. Serve immediately.

Baked chick peas

Garbanzos al horno

6 servings

    2 cups dried chick peas or
    Great Northern beans
    6 cups water
    1 pound salt pork, cut into
    small pieces
    1 medium sized onion, chopped
  ½ teaspoon salt
    1 large bay leaf
  ¼ cup finely chopped parsley
  ½ teaspoon dried thyme
    2 whole cloves
    8 peppercorns, crushed
    1 clove garlic, crushed
    1 tablespoon dry mustard,
    dissolved in 1 tablespoon water
  ¼ cup dark corn syrup

Wash the beans and soak
overnight in cold water if
necessary. Drain the beans.
Place all the ingredients except
the mustard and corn syrup in a
pan and cover with water. Bring
to a boil, cover and simmer
slowly for 3 hours or until the
peas or beans are tender and
the liquid is almost absorbed.
Stir in the mustard and corn
syrup and pour into a buttered
baking dish. Bake uncovered in
a preheated 350° oven for 45
minutes until brown on top.

Pureed chick peas

Garbanzos

4 servings

    1 cup dried chick peas
    1 teaspoon salt
  ½ teaspoon dried coriander
    1 cup diced bacon
    1 medium sized onion, chopped
  ½ cup puréed red chilies
    (canned)
  ¼ to ½ cup hot milk

Cover the chick peas with water
and soak for 24 hours. Drain.
Cover with fresh water, add the
salt and coriander and simmer
gently 1½ hours or until tender.
Fry the bacon until crisp. Add
the onion and fry until soft and
transparent. Drain and mash
the chick peas or purée them in
an electric blender. Add the
bacon fat, bacon, onion and
chilies and blend well. Heat
thoroughly and add hot milk to
the desired consistency.

Pureed yellow peas

Dhal

4 servings

    1 cup dried yellow peas
    3 tablespoons oil
    1 onion, chopped
    3 cloves garlic, crushed
    1 teaspoon ground cumin
    1 teaspoon salt
    Freshly ground black pepper

Soak the peas in water for 24
hours. Drain. Cover with fresh
water and simmer gently until
tender. Drain and force the
cooked peas through a strainer,
or purée in an electric blender.
Heat the oil in a saucepan, add
the onion and garlic and fry for
5 minutes until soft and golden.
Add the puréed peas, cumin,
salt and pepper. Mix well and
cook for 10 minutes, stirring
constantly. Serve with white rice
and roast lamb.

Vegetable stew

Locro

8 servings

2 tablespoons butter
2 onions, finely chopped
2 cloves garlic, crushed
½ cup tomato sauce
½ cup water
1 cup canned corn, drained
1 cup fresh or frozen peas
1 teaspoon salt
   Freshly ground black pepper
4 medium sized potatoes,
   peeled and cut into eighths
1 (16 ounce) can pumpkin
1 cup milk
¾ cup grated Gruyère cheese

Heat the butter in a large saucepan and sauté the onions and garlic until golden brown. Add the tomato sauce, water, corn, peas, salt and pepper and bring to a boil. Lower the heat, cover and simmer 10 minutes. Add the potatoes, pumpkin and milk. Cover and simmer over the lowest possible heat 45 minutes to 1 hour. Stir in the cheese and remove from the heat. Serve with boiled rice.

Latin Americans frequently use seasonal squash and pumpkin to add thickness and color to stew. This version comes from Ecuador.

Zucchini stuffed with corn

Zucchini rellenos

6 servings

- 6 zucchini
- 1 (10 ounce) package frozen corn
- 2 eggs
- 2 tablespoons milk
- ½ teaspoon salt
  Freshly ground black pepper
- ½ cup farmer cheese
- ¼ cup cheddar cheese, grated
- 3 tablespoons butter
- ¾ cup tomato sauce

Trim the zucchini and cut in half lengthwise. Scoop out the seeds and leave a shell about ½ inch thick. Combine the corn, eggs, milk, salt and pepper and beat until smooth, or place in the blender and form a coarse purée. Add the farmer cheese to the corn purée. Fill the zucchini shells with this mixture. Sprinkle with the cheddar cheese and dot with butter. Place in a buttered baking dish. Cover with foil and bake in a preheated 350° oven 45 minutes or until the squash is tender. Pour over the tomato sauce, return to the oven for 10 minutes and serve hot.

Lentils with pineapple

Lentejas con pina

6 servings

- 1½ cups lentils
- ½ cup diced lean bacon
- 2 tablespoons butter
- ½ cup chopped onion
- ¼ teaspoon thyme
- 4 tablespoons tomato catsup
- ½ teaspoon salt
  Freshly ground black pepper
- 1½ cups cubed pineapple (fresh or canned)

Soak the lentils overnight in enough water to cover. Drain. Fry the bacon until crisp. Add the butter and onion and cook until the onion is soft and golden. Add the lentils, thyme and enough water to cover. Bring to a boil, reduce the heat and simmer gently for 1 hour or until the lentils are tender. Drain off any remaining water. Add tomato catsup, salt and pepper. Turn into a buttered ovenproof serving dish. Cover with pineapple cubes. Bake in a preheated 350° oven for 15 minutes.

Spinach with pimiento

Espinaca con pimiento

4 servings

- 2 pounds fresh spinach
- 4 tablespoons olive oil
- 1 clove garlic, crushed
- 1 tablespoon butter
- 1 tablespoon flour
- ⅓ cup milk
- 2 hard boiled eggs, sliced
- 3 large canned pimientos, cut into strips

Wash the spinach thoroughly and shake off the excess water. Heat the olive oil in a saucepan. Add the garlic and spinach and cook, stirring constantly, until the spinach is wilted. Drain and chop the spinach. Heat the butter in a saucepan. Add the flour and cook, stirring, 2 minutes. Add the milk gradually, stirring constantly, until the mixture is very thick. Add the spinach and stir until it is heated through. Transfer to a serving dish and garnish with eggs and pimiento strips.

Candied sweet potatoes and apples

Batata com maçã

4 servings

- 4 large sweet potatoes, cooked and sliced
- 2 large green apples, peeled and sliced
- ¾ cup brown sugar
- ¾ cup chopped walnuts
- 6 tablespoons butter, cut into small pieces
- ½ cup fine dry breadcrumbs

Layer the sweet potatoes and apples in a casserole, sprinkling each layer with the sugar, nuts and 3 tablespoons of the butter. Heat the remaining butter and fry the breadcrumbs 2 minutes. Sprinkle the buttered crumbs over the mixture and bake in a preheated 350° oven for 30 minutes until golden brown.

Green peppers stuffed with eggplant

Pimentões recheados com beringela

4 servings

  4 tablespoons oil
  1 large eggplant, peeled and
     cut into ½ inch cubes
1½ cups tomato sauce (canned
     sauce may be used)
  8 tablespoons grated Parmesan
     cheese
  1 clove garlic, crushed
  2 large green peppers, seeded
     and cut in half

Heat the oil in a frying pan and fry the eggplant until soft. Mix with the tomato sauce, 4 tablespoons of cheese and the garlic. Cook the peppers in salted boiling water for 5 minutes. Drain and fill with the eggplant mixture. Sprinkle the tops with the remaining cheese. Bake in a preheated 350° oven for 20 minutes.

Imaginative preparation of vegetables often serves as the main course of a Brazilian dinner. Here, green peppers are baked with an eggplant filling.

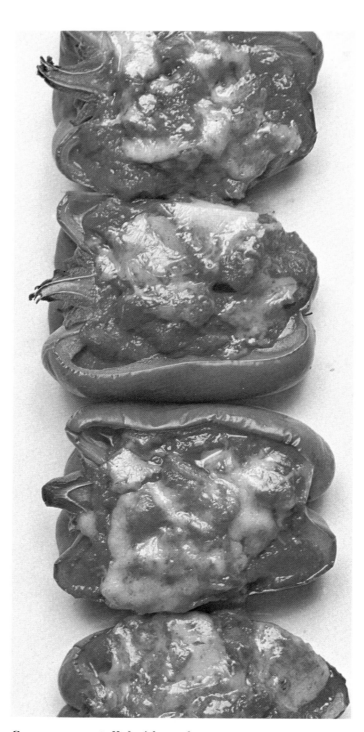

Green peppers stuffed with eggplant

Baked eggplant

Losie boullangé

4 servings

  2 medium sized or 1 very
     large eggplant
  1 tablespoon salt
  3 tablespoons oil
  3 onions, thinly sliced and
     separated into rings
  2 tomatoes, peeled, seeded
     and cut into wedges
 ½ teaspoon salt
     Freshly ground black pepper

To prepare the eggplants, peel and cut into ½ inch thick slices. Sprinkle both sides of the slices with salt and set aside on wire racks for 30 minutes. This will drain the bitter juices from the eggplants. Rinse the slices, pat dry on paper towels and cut into cubes. Oil a casserole with a little of the oil and arrange a layer of onion rings on the bottom. Place a layer of eggplant, then a layer of tomatoes on top. Sprinkle each layer with salt and pepper. Continue layering until all the ingredients are used. Sprinkle the remaining oil over the top. Bake in a 275° oven 1½ hours. Serve from the casserole.

In a land where beauty is weighed by the pound, women most do not worry about adding a little extra fat here and there, so throughout the Latin American countries elaborate sweets are as basic a part of life as bread and water. The native fruits, especially the coconut and the banana, are among features of the sweet scene. One of the happiest sights in Mexico, or any large city, is that of a small boy, or an old woman, balancing a tray of elaborate and carefully prepared sweets, walking throughout the marketplace. In Mexico City there are literally thousands of sweet shops. The Spanish are probably responsible for some of the interesting names applied to the desserts, too : 'Eyes of the Mother-in-law', 'Bones of St. John', 'Royal Eggs', 'Love in Pieces', are but a few. 'Bunuelos' is a kind of generic term for the infinite variety of fried cake sold to accompany coffee in many countries of Latin America.

Pineapple and coconut pudding—see recipe page 78

Pineapple and coconut are blended in a delicious Brazilian pudding that is both sweet and light.

Pineapple and coconut pudding

Pudim de abacaxi e coco

6 servings

- 1 (15 ounce) can condensed milk
- 1⅓ cups milk
- 2 egg yolks, beaten
- 3 tablespoons cornstarch
- ½ teaspoon vanilla
- 1 prepared 9 inch sponge cake layer
- 1 cup pineapple juice
- ⅓ cup rum
- 1 (1 pound 4 ounce) can pineapple slices, drained
- ¾ cup grated coconut
- 1 cup heavy cream, whipped Cherries

Mix the condensed milk, milk, egg yolks, cornstarch and vanilla. Place in a double boiler and cook over hot water, stirring constantly, until thickened. Continue cooking without stirring for 10 minutes. Cool. Cut the sponge cake layer into 2 inch squares and place in the bottom of a serving dish. Mix the pineapple juice and rum and sprinkle over the cake. Cover with ½ the custard mixture. Cut up ½ the pineapple and arrange over the custard. Sprinkle with ½ the coconut. Add a layer of the remaining custard and cover with whipped cream. Decorate with the remaining coconut, pineapple slices and cherries.

Caramel milk dessert

Crema de caramel

6 to 8 servings

- ½ cup raisins
- ¼ cup rum
- 1 (14 ounce) can sweetened condensed milk
- 3 cups milk
- ¼ teaspoon cinnamon
- ¼ teaspoon cloves
- ½ teaspoon baking soda
- 1 cup brown sugar
- ¼ cup water

Soak the raisins in the rum for a hour. Combine the condensed milk, fresh milk, cinnamon, cloves and baking soda. Bring to a boil over high heat, stirring constantly. Remove from the heat. Place the sugar and water in a saucepan. Bring to simmering point, stirring constantly until the sugar dissolves. Pour in the hot milk mixture and mix well. Cook over low heat, stirring occasionally, for 1¼ hours until the pudding is thick and amber colored. Add the rum soaked raisins and refrigerate until well chilled.

Stuffed apples

Pudim de maçã

6 servings

- ⅓ cup flour
- ⅔ cup sugar
- ⅓ cup butter
- 1 teaspoon cinnamon
- 6 large apples, peeled and cored
- ½ cup orange juice
- ¼ cup water
- 1½ cups whipped cream

Combine the flour, sugar, butter and cinnamon. Blend with the fingertips until it resembles breadcrumbs. Fill the center of the apples with ¾ of this mixture and arrange in a buttered baking dish. Sprinkle the remaining mixture on top of the apples. Add the orange juice and water. Bake in a preheated 350° oven for 50 to 60 minutes or until the apples are tender. Serve hot with whipped cream.

Stuffed prunes

Olho de sogra

- 6 tablespoons sugar
- 1 cup water
- 12 egg yolks
- 4 egg whites
- ½ cup ground almonds Few drops vanilla
- 1½ cups powdered sugar
- 1 pound pitted prunes Sugar

Place the sugar and water in a saucepan. Bring to a boil and cook until the sugar dissolves. Beat the egg yolks and egg whites together until well combined. Add the hot syrup slowly, beating constantly with a wire whisk. Return the mixture to the saucepan and cook, stirring constantly until the mixture forms a thick mass. Remove from the heat and stir in the almonds and vanilla. When the mixture is cold, beat in the powdered sugar gradually. Stuff the prunes with the mixture and dredge them in sugar. Wrap each prune in cellophane. These sweets are traditionally served at Brazilian weddings, christenings and birthdays.

Sweet fritters

Bunuelos

6 servings

- 4 tablespoons butter
- ¼ cup sugar
- 2 teaspoons grated lemon rind
- 1 cup water
- 1 cup flour
- 4 eggs
- Oil for deep frying

Sauce:
- 1 cup dark brown sugar
- 3 tablespoons flour
- 1 cup water
- 2 tablespoons heavy cream
- 1 tablespoon butter
- ½ teaspoon vanilla

Combine the butter, sugar, lemon rind and water in a saucepan. Bring to a boil, stirring occasionally. Add the flour all at once, beating hard. Cook about 2 minutes until the dough leaves the sides of the pan. Remove from the heat and add the eggs, 1 at a time. Beat until smooth and shiny. Form balls of the dough with 2 teaspoons and fry in preheated 375° oil for 5 minutes until puffed and lightly browned. Drain on paper towels.
To prepare the sauce, combine the sugar and flour in a saucepan and stir in the water gradually. Cook over medium heat, stirring constantly, until the mixture thickens. Add cream, butter and vanilla and mix well. Serve the hot sauce and fritters separately.

Banana fritters

Beignets de bananes

4 servings

- 6 bananas, peeled and cut into slices
- ½ cup rum
- ½ cup powdered sugar
- 1 teaspoon cinnamon
- 1¼ cups flour
- 1 egg
- 1 tablespoon oil
- 1 cup milk
- ¼ teaspoon salt
- Oil for deep frying
- Powdered sugar

Arrange layers of sliced bananas in a bowl, pouring rum on each layer and sprinkling with sugar and cinnamon. Allow to stand for 30 minutes. Mix the flour, egg, oil, milk and salt and beat well for 2 minutes, or place these ingredients in a blender for form a batter. Coat each banana slice with the batter. Heat the oil to 375° and deep fry the fritters, a few at a time, 3 to 5 minutes until golden brown. Drain on paper towels. Sprinkle with powdered sugar and serve hot.

Pancakes

Arrepa di funchi

6 to 8 servings

- 1½ cups funchi (corn meal)
- 1 cup flour
- ¼ teaspoon salt
- 2 tablespoons sugar
- 2 cups milk
- 3 eggs, beaten
- 2 tablespoons oil
- 1 teaspoon vanilla
- Oil for frying
- Cinnamon sugar

Mix together the corn meal, flour, salt and sugar. Combine the milk, eggs, oil and vanilla. Add to the dry ingredients gradually and beat until smooth. Heat 1 tablespoon oil in a frying pan, cover the surface of the pan with a thin layer of batter and cook for 2 to 3 minutes until lightly browned. Turn and brown on the other side. Sprinkle with cinnamon sugar and keep warm on a serving dish over steaming water. Serve hot with warm applesauce.

Pumpkin fritters

Pilarones

12 servings

- 1 package dry yeast
- ¼ cup lukewarm water
- 2 tablespoons sugar
- 1 egg, lightly beaten
- 1 (16 ounce) can pumpkin
- ½ teaspoon salt
- 4 cups flour
- Oil for deep frying
- Molasses or maple syrup

In a large bowl, sprinkle the yeast over the lukewarm water and stir to dissolve. Add the sugar, egg, pumpkin and salt and combine thoroughly. Add the flour, ½ cup at a time, until the dough becomes too stiff to beat with a spatula. Turn the dough out onto a lightly floured board and knead in enough of the remaining flour to prevent the dough from sticking. You will probably use all of the 4 cups. Continue kneading until the dough is smooth and elastic. Shape it into a ball and place in an oiled bowl. Cover and let rise in a warm place 1 hour or until doubled in bulk. Punch down the dough. Tear off pieces of the dough and shape into doughnut like rings, 3 inches in diameter. Heat the oil for deep frying and fry the fritters about 5 minutes, turning them once, until crisp and golden brown. Drain on paper towels and serve immediately with warm molasses or maple syrup.

Tastes good to me

Bien me sabe

6 to 8 servings

- *1 coconut*
- *2 cups hot water*
- *1 cup sugar*
- *1 (2 inch) stick cinnamon*
- *6 egg yolks*
- *1 prepared sponge cake layer, cut into pieces*
- *¾ cup muscatel wine*
- *1 teaspoon powdered cinnamon*

Drain the liquid from the coconut. Remove the brown skin and grate the coconut meat finely. Place in a fine strainer and pour the hot water over the grated coconut. Allow the water to drip through for about 15 minutes. Press down hard with the back of the spoon to extract 2 cups of coconut milk.

Dissolve the sugar in 1½ cups of the coconut milk. Add the cinnamon stick and cook over moderate heat until the syrup reaches 230° or soft ball stage. Discard the cinnamon stick and remove the pan from the heat. Beat the egg yolks until very thick and lemon colored. Add the remaining ½ cup of coconut milk and beat in 3 tablespoons coconut syrup. Gradually stir the egg yolk mixture into the syrup and cook over low heat, stirring constantly. Do not allow the mixture to boil or the egg yolks will curdle. Place the sponge cake pieces in a serving dish and soak with the wine. Pour on the coconut cream. Chill in the refrigerator for 3 hours. Sprinkle with cinnamon before serving.

Mother in law's dessert

Pudim de sogra

6 servings

- *12 bananas, sliced lengthwise*
- *1 (8 ounce package) cream cheese*
- *1 (14 ounce) can sweetened condensed milk*
- *4 egg whites*
- *½ cup sugar*

Place the sliced bananas in a buttered ovenproof serving dish. Bake in a 350° oven 3 to 5 minutes until the bananas are slightly softened. Beat the cream cheese until light and fluffy. Add the condensed milk and beat until smooth. Spread the mixture over the bananas. Beat the egg whites with the sugar until stiff peaks form. Spoon the meringue over the banana mixture and bake in a 350° oven 10 minutes until the meringue is lightly browned. Serve from the baking dish.

Caramel pudding

Flan

6 servings

- *¼ cup sugar*
- *4 eggs*
- *1 (14 ounce) can sweetened condensed milk*
- *1 cup water*
- *1 teaspoon vanilla*
- *¼ cup dark rum, heated*

Place the sugar in a small heavy saucepan and melt over low heat, stirring constantly. When the sugar turns golden brown, dip the bottom of the saucepan in cold water to stop the cooking. Immediately pour the caramel into a 1 quart ovenproof mold, rolling it around the sides to coat the mold evenly. Beat the eggs until frothy. Combine the condensed milk, water and vanilla and beat the mixture into the eggs. Pour the custard into the caramelized mold. Place the mold in a larger pan and add water to come halfway up the sides of the mold. Bake in a 350° oven 1 to 1¼ hours or until a knife inserted in the center of the custard comes out clean. Cool to room temperature then place in the refrigerator 3 hours. Unmold the flan on a serving plate. Ignite the heated rum, pour it over the flan and bring it to the table flaming.

Desserts in Latin America often have most unusual names – 'arm of the gipsy' – 'nun's sighs' – 'kisses.

Mother in law's dessert

Coconut blancmange

Manjar branco

4 servings

- 1 cup unsweetened grated coconut
- 1 cup boiling water
- 3 cups milk
- ½ cup sugar
- 6 tablespoons cornstarch
- ¼ teaspoon salt
- ½ teaspoon coconut flavoring

Mix the grated coconut and boiling water in a bowl and allow to stand for 15 minutes. Heat the milk and sugar in a saucepan and stir until the sugar is dissolved. Bring to a boil slowly. Strain the coconut liquid, discard the coconut meat and mix the liquid with the cornstarch until smooth. Add ½ cup of the boiling milk. Return to the pan with the remaining milk, add the salt and cook until thickened, stirring constantly. Cook over a low heat for 10 minutes. Add the coconut flavoring, pour into a 4 cup mold rinsed with cold water and refrigerate 3 to 4 hours until set. Unmold onto a serving dish and serve with a compôte of prunes or a chocolate or vanilla sauce.

Coconut provides a delicate sweetness to many dishes in Brazil.

Sweet milk dessert

Dulce de leche

4 servings

- 2 cups milk
- ¾ cup sugar
  Pinch of baking soda
- 1 teaspoon vanilla
- 1 recipe butter cookies (see following recipe)
- 1 cup sweetened coconut

Combine the milk, sugar and baking soda in a saucepan and bring to the boiling point. Lower the heat and barely simmer the mixture 2 to 2½ hours, stirring occasionally. It will thicken and form a soft ball when a small spoonful is dropped into cold water. Remove from the heat and stir in the vanilla. Let the mixture cool a few minutes and spread it on the cookies. Sandwich the cookies together in pairs and roll the edges in grated coconut.

Butter cookies

Alfajores

40 cookies

- ½ cup butter
- 1 cup sugar
- 1 egg
- 2 egg yolks
- 1 teaspoon vanilla
- 1 tablespoon brandy
- 2 teaspoons grated lemon rind
- 1½ cups cornstarch
- ½ cup flour
- 1 teaspoon baking powder
- ¼ teaspoon salt

Beat the butter until creamy. Add the sugar gradually, beating until the mixture is light and fluffy. Add the egg and egg yolks, 1 at a time, beating well after each addition. Beat in the vanilla, brandy and lemon rind. Sift together the cornstarch, flour, baking powder and salt. Gradually add the dry ingredients to the butter mixture, beating until thoroughly combined. Drop the batter by small spoonfuls onto well buttered baking sheets. Leave enough space between the cookies because they will spread. Bake in a 350° oven 15 minutes. Immediately remove from the baking sheets and let cool. Sandwich the cookies together with sweet milk dessert (see previous recipe).

Coconut blancmange

82

Meringue dessert

Postre chaja

6 servings

- 4 egg whites
  Pinch of salt
- ¼ teaspoon cream of tartar
- 1¾ cups sugar
- 1 teaspoon vanilla
- ¼ cup water
- 5 egg yolks
- 1 cup butter
- 1 tablespoon brandy
- 6 (½ inch) slices sponge cake
  or
  12 lady fingers
- 1 cup sliced strawberries
- 1 cup heavy cream, whipped

Beat the egg whites with the salt
and ⅛ teaspoon cream of tartar
until foamy. Add 1 cup sugar
gradually, beating constantly
until stiff peaks form. Beat in
the vanilla. Oil and flour 2
large baking sheets. Form the
meringue into 12 flat rounds,
4 inches in diameter, on the
baking sheets. Bake in a 250°
oven 1 hour. Turn the oven off
and leave the meringues in the
oven several hours or overnight.
Combine the remaining cream
of tartar, sugar and water in a
saucepan. Bring to a boil and
cook until a candy thermometer
registers 230°. Beat the egg yolks
and add the syrup by droplets,
beating constantly. Continue
beating a few minutes to cool
the mixture. Beat the butter until
very light and fluffy and add the
brandy. Beat the butter into the
cooled egg yolk mixture. Spread
each meringue on 1 side with a
very thin layer of butter cream.
To assemble the dessert, place a
slice of sponge cake or 2 lady
fingers on the butter cream side
of each of 6 meringues. Arrange
strawberries on top and spread
with whipped cream. Top with
the remaining meringues, butter
cream side down, and spread the
remaining butter cream on the
top and sides. Crumbled
meringue can be sprinkled on
top as decoration.

Coconut cakes

Mae bentas

Makes 24

- ⅓ cup butter
- 1 cup sugar
- 6 egg yolks
- 1 cup rice flour
- ¼ teaspoon salt
- 1 cup grated coconut
- 4 egg whites, stiffly beaten

Beat the butter and sugar
together in a bowl. Gradually
add the egg yolks and beat until
very light and creamy. Mix
together the rice flour, salt and
coconut and fold into the yolk
mixture. Gently fold in the
stiffly beaten egg whites. Line
muffin pans with paper cases and
fill ⅔ full with the cake mixture.
Bake in a preheated 350° oven
for 25 minutes. Turn out and
cool on a rack.

Coconut pastries

Pastelitos de coco

Pastry:
- 2 cups flour
- ½ teaspoon baking powder
- ½ teaspoon salt
- 8 tablespoons butter
- 4 to 5 tablespoons cold water

Filling:
- 1 tablespoon flour
- ¼ cup sugar
- 1½ cups sweetened flaked coconut
- ¾ cup light cream
- 3 tablespoons butter
- 2 egg yolks, lightly beaten

Glaze:
- 1 egg yolk, lightly beaten

To prepare the pastry, sift the flour, baking powder and salt together into a bowl. Cut the butter into the flour, using a pastry blender or 2 knives until the mixture resembles coarse meal. Add 4 tablespoons water and stir with a fork until the dough can be gathered into a ball. Add more water by droplets if necessary to make the dough stick together. Wrap in waxed paper and refrigerate 1 hour. To prepare the filling, combine 1 tablespoon flour, sugar and coconut in a saucepan. Add the cream and cook over low heat, stirring constantly until the mixture thickens. Stir in the butter and simmer 2 minutes. Reduce the heat to the lowest possible point and add the egg yolks, stirring vigorously. Remove from the heat and let the mixture cool. To assemble the tarts, roll out the pastry on a floured board to a ⅛ inch thickness. Cut it into rounds using a 3 inch cookie cutter. Place 1 tablespoon of the filling on half of the rounds and top with the remaining rounds. Press the edges of the pastry together with a fork to seal. Place the tarts on a buttered baking sheet. Brush with egg yolk and prick with a fork. Bake in a 425° oven 12 minutes until lightly browned.

Coconut candies

Cocadas

Makes about 2 pounds

- 3 cups sugar
- ¾ cup milk
- ½ cup corn syrup
- ¼ teaspoon salt
- 1 tablespoon lemon juice
- 2 cups shredded coconut
- 3 tablespoons butter

Mix the sugar, milk, corn syrup, salt and lemon juice in a saucepan. Heat until the sugar is dissolved, stirring constantly. Bring to a boil, cover and cook for 3 minutes until the steam has dissolved the crystals which may have formed on the sides of the pan. Uncover and cook, without stirring, until a soft ball stage is reached (238° on a candy thermometer). Remove from the heat. Stir in the coconut and butter. Pour into a buttered dish. When cool enough to handle, shape into small balls and leave to harden overnight.

Coconut pie

Torta de coco com crema

6 servings

- 1 (9 inch) prepared unbaked pie shell
- 2 cups milk
- 4 eggs
- ½ cup sugar
- ¼ teaspoon salt
- ½ teaspoon vanilla
- 2 tablespoons butter, melted
- ½ cup grated coconut

Chill the pie shell for 30 minutes before cooking. Scald the milk in a double boiler until bubbles form around the edge. Beat the eggs and add the sugar, salt, vanilla, butter and coconut. Stir in the scalded milk. Pour into the chilled pie shell. Bake in a preheated 400° oven for 25 to 30 minutes or until the custard is set to within ½ inch of the center. Chill the pie for 4 hours before serving.

Coconut pastries *Little tarts filled with delicate coconut cream and beautifully glazed are typical of Bolivian sweets.*

84

Mexicans love chocolate – in all forms. This is a rich, flaky pastry concoction for a special fiesta treat.

Chocolate torte—see recipe page 85

Chocolate torte

Torta de chocolate

Pastry:
1½ cups flour
½ cup cocoa
½ teaspoon salt
1 cup butter
⅓ cup sour cream

Filling:
16 ounces semi-sweet chocolate
¼ cup cream
½ cup butter
5 egg yolks
1 teaspoon vanilla

To prepare the pastry, sift the flour, cocoa and salt together into a bowl. Cut the butter into the flour mixture with a pastry blender or 2 knives until it resembles coarse meal. Add the sour cream and knead into a ball. Divide into 4 equal pieces and refrigerate 2 hours. On a floured board, roll each piece of dough out to a 10 × 10 inch square. Place each square on a buttered baking sheet, prick all over with a fork and bake in a 400° oven 10 minutes. Carefully transfer the pastry squares to wire racks to cool. They will be very fragile.
To prepare the filling, place the chocolate, cream and butter in a saucepan and stir over low heat until the chocolate and butter are melted. Beat the egg yolks until thick. Beat in a few tablespoons of the hot chocolate mixture and stir back into the hot chocolate. Stir in the vanilla and let the mixture cool to spreading consistency. Do not refrigerate or it will be too stiff to spread. Place 1 pastry layer on a serving plate and spread with the filling. Continue layering.

Layered sponge cake

Pavé

6 to 8 servings

1 cup sugar
¾ cup water
4 egg yolks
¾ cup powdered sugar
½ pound sweet butter
1 (6 ounce) package semi sweet chocolate pieces
⅓ cup water
16 (2 packages) lady fingers
½ cup port wine or sherry
½ cup toasted slivered almonds

Place the sugar and water in a saucepan. Bring to a boil, and continue cooking until the syrup reaches 230° on the candy thermometer (soft ball stage). Beat the egg yolks until light and thick. Add the powdered sugar and continue beating until very thick and fluffy. Add the boiled syrup in a thin steady stream to the egg yolk mixture, beating constantly. Set aside to cool. Beat the butter until soft and combine with the cooled egg yolk mixture. Melt the chocolate pieces in the water and stir until smooth. Add to the butter cream. Arrange 8 halves of lady fingers in a 9 × 5 inch pan that has been lined with waxed paper. Sprinkle 2 tablespoons wine over the lady fingers and cover with a layer of the chocolate cream. Repeat this procedure 3 more times, reserving enough cream to cover the sides. Refrigerate for 2 hours. Remove the waxed paper and transfer to a serving dish. Cover the sides with the chocolate cream and decorate with almonds. Refrigerate 12 hours before serving.

Raisin cake

Torta de pasa

8 servings

1 tablespoon cornstarch
½ cup water
¾ cup sugar
1 cup seedless raisins
½ cup chopped nuts
½ cup butter
½ cup dark brown sugar
2 eggs, beaten
2 cups flour
1½ teaspoons cream of tartar
1½ teaspoons baking soda
½ cup milk
1 teaspoon vanilla

Mix the cornstarch and water in a saucepan until smooth. Add ½ cup of the sugar and cook over low heat, stirring constantly, until thickened. Add the raisins and nuts and set aside while preparing the batter. Beat the butter until soft and fluffy. Add the brown sugar and remaining white sugar and continue beating until thick and light in color. Add the eggs and beat well. Sift the flour, cream of tartar and baking soda together and add alternately with the milk. Add the vanilla and mix well. Pour ½ the batter into a buttered 8 inch square pan. Spread with the raisin mixture and cover with the remaining batter. Bake in a preheated 350° oven for 40 minutes or until a cake tester comes out clean. Cool. Turn out of the pan and cut into squares.

Egg cake

Huevos reales

6 to 8 servings

2 tablespoons seedless raisins
½ cup cream sherry
2 egg whites
8 egg yolks
1 tablespoon butter
1½ cups sugar
½ cup water
1 (2 inch) stick cinnamon
¼ cup slivered toasted almonds

Soak the raisins in the sherry for 1 hour. Beat the egg whites until stiff. Beat the egg yolks until very thick and light yellow. Fold the egg whites into the yolks. Pour the egg yolk mixture into a buttered 8 inch square pan, set in a baking pan of boiling water, and bake in a preheated 325° oven for 15 minutes or until the egg cake is firmly set. Cool and cut into 2 inch squares with a heated knife. Dissolve the sugar in the water, add the cinnamon stick and boil briskly for 5 minutes. Strain the sherry from the raisins and add to the sugar syrup. Remove the cinnamon stick. Soak the egg squares in the syrup and arrange on a serving dish. Pour the remaining strained syrup over the egg squares and decorate with raisins and slivered almonds.

Cocoa cakes

Pasteles de cacao

16 cakes

½ cup butter
1 cup sugar
3 eggs
¾ cup cocoa
1½ cups flour
3 teaspoons baking powder
 Pinch of salt
⅔ cup milk
1 teaspoon vanilla

Beat the butter until creamy. Add the sugar, gradually beating until the mixture is light and fluffy. Add the eggs, 1 at a time, beating well after each addition. Sift together the cocoa, flour, baking powder and salt. Add the dry ingredients alternately with the milk, beating just until the flour is thoroughly incorporated. Beat in the vanilla. Spoon the batter into buttered and floured muffin tins, filling each cup ⅔ full. Bake the cakes in a 375° oven 20 minutes or until a cake tester comes out clean. Carefully remove the cakes from the muffin tins and cool on wire racks. They may be served warm or cold.

Almond pudding

Almendrado

4 to 6 servings

1 package unflavored gelatin
1¼ cups water
1 cup powdered sugar
5 egg whites
½ teaspoon almond extract
½ cup ground almonds

Soften the gelatin in ¼ cup cold water. Bring the remaining water to a boil, add the sugar and stir until dissolved. Remove from the heat. Add the softened gelatin and allow to cool until it begins to set. Beat the egg whites until stiff and shiny. Combine the gelatin and egg white mixture with the almond extract and ground almonds. Turn into a 6 cup mold and refrigerate until firm. Unmold and serve with chilled sauce.

Sauce:

¼ cup masa harina (corn flour)
1 cup water
1 (2 inch) cinnamon stick
⅓ cup sugar
⅓ cup ground almonds
2 cups milk
2 egg yolks, beaten

Stir the masa harina into the water. Add the cinnamon stick and bring to a boil, stirring constantly until it thickens. Add the sugar, almonds and milk. Stir until the mixture begins to boil again. Pour ¼ cup of the hot mixture onto the egg yolks and mix well. Add the egg yolk mixture to the milk and cook slowly for 2 minutes. Remove the cinnamon stick and refrigerate.

Masa harina is a corn meal made from dehydrated cooked corn and is available in Spanish markets.

Cocoa cakes

Chocolate is a famous Latin American product – and is used in a multitude of ways throughout the land. Here, it is baked into little cakes to serve with excellent Colombian coffee.

South America produces most of the coffee of the world – and its care and preparation has become a fine art – particularly in Brazil and Colombia, the two giants among the coffee producers. Latin Americans sneer at 'American' coffee, preferring instead the thick, sweet infusion which they drink by the thimbleful, as often as twenty times a day. Chocolate is a great favorite in Mexico – hot and sweet. And the variety of highly colored, richly sweetened soft drinks consumed throughout Latin America is awesome to behold.

Wine, from grapes first introduced by the Spaniards, is becoming of increasing importance throughout South America. Chile and Argentina lead in production of some excellent vintages. Mexico is known for 'pulque', a mildly alcoholic drink, excellent beer, and best of all for tequila – a

distillation of the agave plant, a member of the cactus family. Rum is used freely in both cooking and drinking and each country has a favorite brandy distillation – with the Pisco of Peru an outstanding favorite. Herbal teas and infusions of chocolate, cinnamon and sugar are the common beverages in the home. Politeness dictates the custom of offering a visitor at least one kind of liquid refreshment, and it is considered an insult to refuse whatever is offered. Coca-Cola is ubiquitous. Lemonade is popular and the variety of fruit punches, both alcoholic and nonalcoholic, are almost limitless.

Truly, the people of Latin America care about food – they regard it not only as essential for survival, but in its preparation and presentation, it becomes a way of life in itself. Look at it! Learn from it! Enjoy it!

Spicy coffee

Café temperado

4 servings

- 3 cups strong hot coffee, made with 7 teaspoons soluble coffee
- 2 vanilla beans, split in half lengthwise
- 4 cloves
  Fresh cream
  Crushed ice
  Sugar to taste

Pour the hot coffee over the vanilla beans and cloves and allow to infuse for 1 hour. Strain the coffee and pour over cream and crushed ice in individual glasses. Add sugar to taste.

Chocolate milk

Chocolate con leche

6 servings

- 4 cups milk
- 4 ounces Mexican chocolate, grated
- 1 egg yolk
- ½ cup cream
- 2 tablespoons sugar
- ½ teaspoon cinnamon
- ¼ teaspoon nutmeg

Heat ½ cup of the milk, add the grated chocolate and stir until dissolved. Add the remaining milk and bring slowly to a boil. Mix the egg yolk with the cream, sugar, cinnamon and nutmeg. Stir well and add to the hot chocolate milk, stirring constantly. Bring almost to boiling point. Remove from the heat and beat with a wire whisk until a thick layer of foam has formed on the surface. Serve immediately.

Rum cocktail

Caipirinha

4 servings

> *Juice of 2 lemons*
> *4 tablespoons sugar*
> *Crushed ice*
> *4 jiggers pinga or rum*

Mix the lemon juice and sugar together in a shaker or stir until the sugar is dissolved. Add the crushed ice and rum and shake until well blended. Serve with crushed ice.
The main drink in Brazil is called "Cachaca" or "Pinga." This is refined cane alcohol which is now being imported into the U.S.A. If it is not available, Bacardi, a light white rum, may be used. The drink in this recipe is called Caipirinha, when it is made with pinga, and Caipirissima, when it is made with rum.

Spiced rum punch

Quentão

8 to 12 servings

> *4 cups boiling water*
> *2 cups rum*
> *6 cloves*
> *1 vanilla bean*
> *2 cups sugar*
> *2 thin slices ginger root*

Add all the ingredients to the boiling water. Cover and allow to infuse for 30 minutes. Strain and reheat. Serve, piping hot in glasses or earthenware mugs.

This is a hot spicy drink, traditionally served in midwinter during the São Joao celebrations (the national thanksgiving and fireworks festival).

Lemon crash

Batida de limão

6 to 8 servings

> *2 cups rum*
> *1 very large lemon, including the rind, cut into pieces and seeds removed*
> *2 to 3 tablespoons sugar*
> *4 ice cubes, crushed*

Place all the ingredients in the jar of an electric blender and blend at low speed several minutes until the lemon is very finely chopped. Strain into a pitcher, pressing down on the lemon pieces to extract all the liquid. Chill 1 hour before serving.
This drink may be made with passion fruit (Batida de maracuja) or coconut (Batida de coco) in place of the lemon. When using coconut, the sugar may be replaced by condensed milk.

Tomato crash

Batida de tomate

6 servings

> *3 large ripe tomatoes, peeled, seeded and chopped*
> *6 jiggers light rum*
> *6 tablespoons dry Marsala*
> *6 tablespoons sugar*
> *Juice of 2 limes*
> *½ cup crushed ice*

Place all the ingredients in the jar of an electric blender and blend until smooth.
Serve over ice.

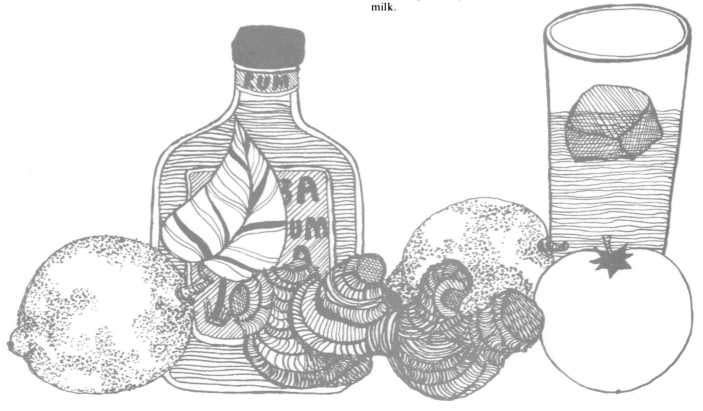

Brazilian punch

Ponche Brasiliero

50 servings

2 cups strong Mate (herb tea)
1 cup lemon juice
4 cups orange juice
2 cups brandy
2 bottles dry white wine
2 bottles club soda
   Sugar to taste

Make the tea and allow it to brew for 10 minutes. Strain and discard the leaves. Mix with the remaining ingredients except the soda water and sugar. Chill in the refrigerator until ready to serve. Pour into a punch bowl over ice cubes. Add the soda water and sugar to taste.

This punch uses the famous Mate, an herb tea drunk daily in the south of Brazil and in Argentina. Traditionally, it is drunk out of Bombillas (a hollow gourd) and sucked through a silver tube with a spoon-shaped strainer on the end.

Sangrita

Sangrita

4 servings

1 cup tomato juice
3 tablespoons orange juice
4 tablespoons lemon juice
   Dash of salt
   Drop of onion juice
   Few drops tabasco sauce
6 ounces tequila

Place the tomato juice, orange juice, lemon juice, salt, onion juice and tabasco sauce in a cocktail shaker. Shake vigorously and chill the mixture thoroughly. Place 3 ice cubes in each of 4 glasses and add the tequila. Fill the glasses with the tomato juice mixture and serve immediately.

Sangria

Sangria

8 to 12 servings

3 fresh peaches, peeled and
   thinly sliced
2 apples, cored and thinly
   sliced
2 bottles red wine
   Sugar, if desired
¼ cup gin (optional)
   Ice cubes

Place the peaches and apples in a glass jug and pour in the wine. A few teaspoons of sugar may be added if a sweeter drink is preferred, though it is not normally done. Add the gin if you would like a stronger drink. Add plenty of ice cubes and stir gently with a wooden spoon until the wine is thoroughly chilled.

This is a favorite Argentinian drink and an effective thirst quencher. The country has many good red wines which serve as a base for sangria.

Eggnog

El ponche crema

4 servings

4 eggs, separated
1 cup sweetened condensed
milk
1 cup rum

Beat the egg yolks until thick
and creamy. Beat the egg
whites until stiff and fold
into the yolks. Add the
condensed milk and mix
thoroughly. Add the rum and
cool in the refrigerator until
well chilled. Serve very cold.

Yucatan

Yucatan

2 servings

1 jigger pineapple juice
½ jigger crème de menthe
1 jigger tequila
Crushed ice
2 small pieces of pineapple
2 green maraschino cherries

Pour the pineapple juice,
crème de menthe and tequila
into a cocktail shaker and add
crushed ice. Shake well and
serve in cocktail glasses.
Decorate with a piece of
pineapple and a green
maraschino cherry.

Tequila cocktail

Margarita

4 servings

2 lemon wedges
Coarse salt
2 ounces fresh lemon juice
6 ounces tequila
2 ounces Triple Sec
Ice cubes

Rub the rims of 4 cocktail
glasses with lemon wedges and
coat with coarse salt. Place the
remaining ingredients in a
cocktail shaker and shake
vigorously several times. Strain
into the prepared cocktail
glasses and serve.

Pisco sour

Pisco

6 servings

6 (1½ ounce) jiggers Pisco
1 jigger sugar syrup or honey
1 jigger lemon juice
½ teaspoon bitters
1 egg white
Crushed ice

Place the Pisco, sugar syrup,
lemon juice and bitters in a
cocktail shaker and stir to mix.
Add the egg white and crushed
ice and shake vigorously.
Strain into cocktail glasses
and serve.

Aspic
A stiff gelatine obtained by combining fish or meat bouillon with gelatine powder.

Au gratin
Obtained by covering a dish with a white sauce (usually prepared with grated cheese) and then heating the dish in the oven so that a golden crust forms.

Baste
To moisten meat or other foods while cooking to add flavor and to prevent drying of the surface. The liquid is usually melted fat, meat drippings, fruit juice or sauce.

Blanch (precook)
To preheat in boiling water or steam. (1) Used to inactivate enzymes and shrink food for canning, freezing, and drying. Vegetables are blanched in boiling water or steam, and fruits in boiling fruit juice, sirup, water, or steam. (2) Used to aid in removal of skins from nuts, fruits, and some vegetables.

Blend
To mix thoroughly two or more ingredients.

Bouillon
Brown stock, conveniently made by dissolving a bouillon cube in water.

Broth
Water in which meat, fish or vegetables have been boiled or cooked.

'En papillote'
Meat, fish or vegetables wrapped in grease-proof paper or aluminum foil (usually first sprinkled with oil or butter, herbs and seasonings) and then baked in the oven or grilled over charcoal. Most of the taste and aroma are preserved in this way.

Fold
To combine by using two motions, cutting vertically through the mixture and turning over and over by sliding the implement across the bottom of the mixing bowl with each turn.

Fry
To cook in fat; applied especially (1) to cooking in a small amount of fat, also called sauté or pan-fry; (2) to cooking in a deep layer of fat, also called deep-fat frying.

Marinate
To let food stand in a marinade usually an oil–acid mixture like French dressing.

Parboil
To boil until partially cooked. The cooking is usually completed by another method.

Poach
To cook in a hot liquid using precautions to retain shape. The temperature used varies with the food.

Reduce
To concentrate the taste and aroma of a particular liquid or food e.g. wine, bouillon, soup, sauce etc. by boiling in a pan with the lid off so that the excess water can evaporate.

Roast
To cook, uncovered, by dry heat. Usually done in an oven, but occasionally in ashes, under coals or on heated stones or metals. The term is usually applied to meats but may refer to other food as potatoes, corn, chestnuts.

Sauté
To brown or cook in a small amount of fat. See Fry.

Simmer
To cook in a liquid just below the boiling point, at temperatures of 185°–210°. Bubbles form slowly and collapse below the surface.

Skim
To take away a layer of fat from soup, sauces, etc.

Stock
The liquid in which meat or fish has been boiled together with herbs and vegetables.

Whip
To beat rapidly to produce expansion, due to incorporation of air as applied to cream, eggs, and gelatin dishes.

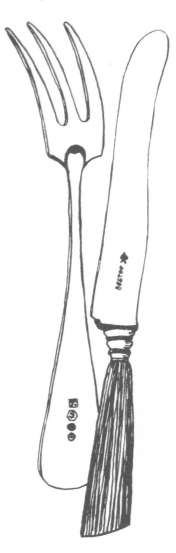

Conversion tables

Liquid measures

American
standard cup | metric equivalent
(approximately)

1 cup = $\frac{1}{2}$ pint	= 8 fl. oz. (fluid ounce)	= 2,37 dl (deciliter)
1 tbs. (tablespoon)	= $\frac{1}{2}$ fl. oz.	= 1,5 cl (centiliter)
1 tsp. (teaspoon)	= $\frac{1}{6}$ fl. oz.	= 0,5 cl
1 pint	= 16 fl. oz.	= 4,73 dl
1 quart = 2 pints	= 32 fl. oz.	= 9,46 dl

British
standard cup | metric equivalent
(approximately)

1 cup = $\frac{1}{2}$ pint	= 10 fl. oz.	= 2,84 dl
1 tbs.	= 0.55 fl. oz.	= 1,7 cl
1 tsp.	= $\frac{1}{5}$ fl. oz.	= 0,6 cl
1 pint	= 20 fl. oz.	= 5,7 dl
1 quart = 2 pints	= 40 fl. oz.	= 1,1 l (liter)

1 cup = 16 tablespoons
1 tablespoon = 3 teaspoons

1 liter = 10 deciliter = 100 centiliter

Solid measures

American/British
| | | metric equivalent
(approximately) |

1 lb. (pound)	= 16 oz. (ounces)	= 453 g (gram)
	1 oz.	= 28 g
2.2 lbs.		= 1000 g = 1 kg (kilogram)
	$3\frac{1}{2}$ oz.	= 100 g

Oven temperatures

Centigrade	Fahrenheit	
up to 105° C	up to 225° F	cool
105–135° C	225–275° F	very slow
135–160° C	275–325° F	slow
175–190° C	350–375° F	moderate
215–230° C	400–450° F	hot
230–260° C	450–500° F	very hot
260° C	500° F	extremely hot

94

Meat dishes

55 Barbecued meat (Peru)
59 Beef creole (Uruguay)
61 Boiled meat (Argentina)
63 Brazilian stew (Brazil)
61 Creole stew (Argentina)
58 Fillet of beef Mar del
   Plata style (Argentina)
59 Fried pastries with meat
   filling (Brazil)
63 Leg of lamb Mexican
   style (Mexico)
57 Meat balls (Uruguay)
56 Meat balls (Mexico)
57 Meat balls in almond
   sauce (Mexico)
56 Meat balls with herbs
   (Mexico)
60 Pepper pork (Bolivia)
60 Pickled and fried
   spareribs (Peru)
60 Pork and chicken
   (Columbia)
61 Pork stew with vegetables
   and fruit (Mexico)
58 Rolled stuffed flank steak
   (Argentina)
63 Spiced loin of pork
   (Mexico)
64 Spicy meat pie (Mexico)
57 Steak with Huancaina
   sauce (Peru)
57 Steak with peanut sauce
   (Colombia)
55 Stewed meat with onions
   and raisins (Cuba)

Poultry and game

70 Chicken and rice
   (Guyanas)

70 Chicken hunter's style
   (Colombia)
71 Chicken in nut sauce
   (Mexico)
66 Chicken in orange juice
   and pineapple (Mexico)
70 Chicken in pepper sauce
   (Ecuador)
67 Chicken livers in sauce
   (Antilles)
69 Chicken, shrimp and rice
   (Guyanas)
66 Chicken with
   mushrooms (Antilles)
66 Fried chicken
   (Dominican Republic)
65 Peppered chicken (Peru)
67 Rice with chicken
   (Dominican Republic)
67 Squabs stuffed with
   noodles (Chile)
71 Turkey casserole
   (Uruguay)
71 Turkey in chocolate sauce
   (Mexico)
71 Turkey in green sauce
   (Mexico)
69 Venezuelan chicken in
   vinegar (Venezuela)

Vegetable dishes

73 Baked chick peas
   (Argentina)
76 Baked eggplant
   (Guyanas)
73 Brown beans with rice
   (Dutch Guyana)
75 Candied sweet potatoes
   and apples (Brazil)
76 Green peppers stuffed
   with eggplant (Brazil)

75 Lentils with pineapple
   (Mexico)
72 Potatoes with cheese and
   onion sauce (Peru)
73 Puréed chick peas
   (Mexico)
73 Puréed yellow peas
   (Trinidad)
72 Refried beans (Mexico)
75 Spinach with pimiento
   (Mexico)
74 Vegetable stew
   (Ecuador)
75 Zucchini stuffed with
   corn (Mexico)

Desserts

86 Almond pudding
   (Mexico)
79 Banana fritters
   (Martinique)
81 Butter cookies
   (Argentina)
78 Caramel milk dessert
   (Peru)
80 Caramel pudding
   (Mexico)
85 Chocolate torte (Mexico)
86 Cocoa cakes (Colombia)
81 Coconut blancmange
   (Brazil)
82 Coconut cakes (Brazil)
83 Coconut candies (Brazil)
83 Coconut pastries
   (Bolivia)
83 Coconut pie (Brazil)
85 Egg cake (Mexico)
85 Layered sponge cake
   (Brazil)
82 Meringue dessert
   (Uruguay)

80 Mother in law's dessert
   (Brazil)
79 Pancakes (Antilles)
78 Pineapple and coconut
   pudding (Brazil)
79 Pumpkin fritters (Peru)
85 Raisin cake (Peru)
78 Stuffed apples (Brazil)
78 Stuffed prunes (Brazil)
79 Sweet fritters (Ecuador)
81 Sweet milk dessert
   (Argentina)
80 Tastes good to me
   (Venezuela)

Beverages

89 Brazilian punch (Brazil)
87 Chocolate milk (Mexico)
90 Eggnog (Venezuela)
88 Lemon crash (Brazil)
90 Pisco sour (Peru)
88 Rum cocktail (Brazil)
89 Sangria (Argentina)
89 Sangrita (Mexico)
88 Spiced rum punch
   (Brazil)
87 Spicy coffee (Brazil)
90 Tequila cocktail (Mexico)
88 Tomato crash (Brazil)
90 Yucatan (Mexico)

Alphabetical index

56 Meat balls with herbs (Mexico)
82 Meringue dessert (Uruguay)
42 Mexican corn pie (Mexico)
27 Mixed salad (Mexico)
26 Molded pineapple salad (Brazil)
41 Molded rice (Brazil)
50 Molded salt cod with shrimp sauce (Brazil)
80 Mother in law's dessert (Brazil)

42 Noodles with mushroom sauce (Paraguay)

39 Pancakes with cheese (Brazil)
35 Parsley sauce (Mexico)
33 Peanut soup (Guyanas)
33 Peanut soup (Bolivia)
26 Peasant salad (Chile)
60 Pepper pork (Bolivia)
65 Peppered chicken (Peru)
46 Peruvian pickled fish (Peru)
60 Pickled and fried spareribs (Peru)
45 Pickled fish (Mexico)
47 Pickled mackerel (Uruguay)
46 Pickled raw fish (Peru)
78 Pineapple and coconut pudding (Brazil)
90 Pisco sour (Peru)

60 Pork and chicken (Colombia)
61 Pork stew with vegetables and fruit (Mexico)
72 Potatoes with cheese and onion sauce (Peru)
30 Potato soup (Ecuador)
79 Pumpkin fritters (Peru)
73 Puréed chick peas (Mexico)
73 Puréed yellow peas (Trinidad)

85 Raisin cake (Peru)
72 Refried beans (Mexico)
41 Rice Mexican style (Mexico)
38 Rice pancake (Venezuela)
67 Rice with chicken (Dominican Republic)
43 Rice with ham and pineapple (Jamaica)
41 Rice with sour cream (Mexico)
58 Rolled stuffed flank steak (Argentina)
88 Rum cocktail (Brazil)

89 Sangria (Argentina)
89 Sangrita (Mexico)
53 Shrimp and scallop stew (Chile)
52 Shrimp Bahia style in tomato sauce (Brazil)
51 Shrimp in almond sauce (Ecuador)
51 Shrimp in curry sauce (Guyanas)

50 Shrimp pie (Brazil)
35 Shrimp sauce (Brazil)
33 Shrimp soup 1 (Peru)
33 Shrimp soup 2 (Peru)
63 Spiced loin of pork (Mexico)
88 Spiced rum punch (Brazil)
36 Spicy chocolate sauce (Mexico)
87 Spicy coffee (Brazil)
64 Spicy meat pie (Mexico)
32 Spinach soup with shrimp (Guyanas)
75 Spinach with pimiento (Mexico)
67 Squabs stuffed with noodles (Chile)
57 Steak with Huancaina sauce (Peru)
57 Steak with peanut sauce (Colombia)
55 Stewed meat with onions and raisins (Cuba)
78 Stuffed apples (Brazil)
40 Stuffed corn husks (Mexico)
40 Stuffed corn husks (Uruguay)
27 Stuffed cucumber salad (Brazil)
49 Stuffed fish (Mexico)
25 Stuffed green peppers (Brazil)
78 Stuffed prunes (Brazil)
23 Stuffed roast beef rolls (Mexico)
53 Stuffed squid (Argentina)

79 Sweet fritters (Ecuador)
81 Sweet milk dessert (Argentina)

39 Tacos with chicken (Mexico)
80 Tastes good to me (Venezuela)
88 Tequila cocktail (Mexico)
88 Tomato crash (Brazil)
31 Tortilla soup (Mexico)
37 Tortillas 1 (Mexico)
37 Tortillas 2 (Mexico)
38 Tortillas Acapulco style (Mexico)
38 Tortillas Guadalajara style (Mexico)
38 Tortillas with eggs farmhouse style (Mexico)
71 Turkey casserole (Uruguay)
71 Turkey in chocolate sauce (Mexico)
71 Turkey in green sauce (Mexico)

74 Vegetable stew (Ecuador)
36 Venezuelan barbecue sauce (Venezuela)
69 Venezuelan chicken in vinegar (Venezuela)

30 Watercress soup (Brazil)

90 Yucatan (Mexico)

75 Zucchini stuffed with corn (Mexico)